# Crypto For Conservatives

## Finding Real Value in a Sea of Speculation

Nick Watts

ISBN:
978-0-6489087-4-6 (eBook)
978-0-6489087-5-3 (paperback)

Want to learn more? Visit
cryptoforconservatives.com

# Disclaimer

Cryptography and cryptocurrency are extremely complex topics. This book may contain inaccuracies, either due to the constantly changing nature of the cryptocurrency landscape or due to mistakes on the part of the author. The author does not warrant the accuracy or completeness of the content, nor the reliability of any advice, opinion, statement or other information found within this book or any related materials. Any reliance on such advice, opinions, statements or other information shall be at your sole risk.

The author reserves the right to correct any errors or omissions in any portion of this book at any time in the future without notice.

The information contained within this book is made available without any representation or warranty, express or implied, including warranties of merchantability, non-infringement, or fitness for a particular purpose.

The information in this book is intended for general educational purposes only. It is not intended as financial advice and should not be understood as such.

# Table of Contents

# A Brief History of Money

Cryptocurrency is money. Or at the very least, it is trying to *become* money. Therefore, in order to understand the place of cryptocurrency in the economy and financial markets, we first need to understand some things about money in general. For readers who are gold bugs (or familiar with the Austrian school of economics) some of this material will likely be familiar. But we need to cover it so that we can apply the same core concepts when we come to evaluate various cryptocurrencies.

# Gold and Silver

For thousands of years, civilisations from across the world have recognised gold and silver as "money". The are several reasons why gold and silver have been so widely adopted.

- They are **recognisable** – people know what they are and what they look like.

- They are **portable** – they're light in weight relative to their usual trading value (which makes them easy to carry around between buying and selling locations).

- They are **divisible** – easy to melt down and recombine into more useful weights and sizes.

- They are **fungible** – one ounce of the metal is basically equal to any other ounce (mainly because they can easily be melted down).

- They are **durable** – they are extremely resistant to decay, so they hold their value over long periods of time.

- The are **scarce** – they are difficult to mine out of the ground, so there isn't much danger that the supply level will suddenly shoot up and reduce the purchasing power of your savings.

These properties caused gold and silver to emerge as the most common "medium of exchange" in world commerce. At one time it was possible for people to trade with each other by directly bartering goods. You could offer three loaves of bread to Fred in exchange for his fish. But as more and more people get involved, the economy becomes more complex and bartering becomes more difficult. If I have fish and I want a pair of boots, I need to find someone who has boots and wants fish. Or else I need to do a series of exchanges until I can get hold of the thing that the person with the boots wants to receive from me.

To solve this problem, people naturally gravitate towards whatever commodity is the easiest to exchange later. If I trade my fish for gold or silver, then I can hold on to that gold or silver until I am ready to trade for something else. I can be fairly confident that the person who has what I need will be willing to accept my gold or silver in exchange.

This is how "money" first comes to be in circulation. People trade with each other until one type of commodity naturally emerges as the most convenient medium of exchange.

There is nothing magical about gold or silver. They are *not* universal money. Historical research done by the economist Carl Menger led him to conclude that in many parts of the ancient world the most common commodity in exchange was actually cattle. People were using cattle as money, operating on a "cattle standard"[1]. It is a well known phenomenon that many prison inmates hoard cigarettes, even if they do not personally smoke, because cigarettes emerge as the *de facto* form of money inside the prison.

Money can be anything. It could be salt, honey, tulips, tobacco or countless other things. Whatever commodity is the most convenient for people to exchange in a given context, that is what they will

---

1   Carl Menger, *Principles of Economics*, 263

tend to use as money. However, history shows us that developed societies have repeatedly gravitated towards gold and silver over many centuries. For this reason, gold and silver have become the benchmark by which all other forms of money are measured.

Gold and silver displaced cattle for several reasons. Cattle are perishable. If you save your wealth in cattle, then the cattle may get sick or be attacked by wild animals. The cattle need a food supply. They also need a farmer who will make sure that the herd continually produces offspring to replace the older cattle that die off. Gold and silver do not need this kind of care. You only need a relatively small amount of space where you can keep your gold and silver secure (like a bank vault). You don't need whole fields. You can store your gold and silver for an unlimited amount of time with no requirement for maintenance. Even gold that sinks to the bottom of the salty ocean does not rust or spoil.

Just as gold and silver displaced cattle by being more convenient, if a new type of money were to displace gold and silver, it would need to be even more convenient than those metals in at least some of its attributes. That is what led people to start using paper money.

# Paper Money

Even though gold and silver are lightweight and portable relative to cattle, they do still have some weight to them, which can be frustrating to deal with. Gold and silver are also easier to divide than cattle (a cow must be killed in order to be split in half). But that does not mean that dividing gold and silver has no cost at all. Minting gold and silver bullion into coins takes work. Melting those coins down again to use in jewellery or industry takes even more work.

Paper money can be used to solve a lot of these inconveniences. Paper money is not used as a commodity directly. In the past, when people traded with paper money, they were not giving each other the paper itself in exchange for goods or services. They paper was just an IOU. It represented a *claim* on gold and silver that was stored in a vault somewhere.

By transacting with paper claims on gold and silver, much of the cost and inconvenience of carrying physical metal was eliminated. Over time, people became accustomed to this way of doing things. Many people stopped bothering to hold any physical gold and silver at all. Instead, they chose to save their money in more convenient paper forms, letting someone else worry about storing and transporting the physical metal. Eventually, transactions conducted with paper money became even more common than transactions conducted with physical gold and silver. Paper claims circulated so widely that many people came to act as though the paper claims themselves were truly money (rather than IOUs pointing to the *real* money in the vaults).

This paved the way for a new era, the period of "fiat" paper money. That is, paper money that does not give the owner a claim to anything else. It's just paper. That is where we are today.

## Inflation: How Government Ruins Everything

As society moves on from one type of money to the next, one thing remains constant. The government always finds a way to inflate the money supply. This has been done in many different ways, depending on the type of money being used at the time. But the basic idea is always the same and has predictable effects.

What is "inflation"? It is simply when the government artificially increases the number of units of money that are circulating in the economy. For example, suppose that a group of people were using gold coins as their primary money. To inflate the money supply, the government could create a large batch of new coins made out of some other, cheaper metal and then coat them with gold so that they looked like real gold coins. They could then go and spend these counterfeit coins as if they were real. At first, they could use these coins to buy just as many goods and services as they could have bought with real gold coins. Over time, society would adjust to the fact that there were more coins circulating. Because there were more coins circulating, people would be able to bid five coins for a service that previously would cost three coins. Prices of different goods and services would then go up until they reached a new equilibrium to reflect the larger number of circulating coins.

In that sense, "inflation" is just another word for "counterfeiting money". Governments have successfully convinced most people that they have a right to do this, even though it would be a crime for anyone else. But the results of "inflation" and "counterfeiting" are exactly the same.

## The Effects of Inflation

Inflation has three primary effects. First, inflation redistributes wealth through the so-called "Cantillon effect". Second, inflation sets the boom-bust cycle in motion in the economy. Third, inflation eventually forces the society to adopt a new monetary standard.

## The Cantillon Effect

The Cantillon effect is named after a famous economist, Richard Cantillon. In simple terms, the Cantillon effect is when wealth is transferred from one group to another because of the time it takes for new money to work its way through the economy.

The simplest way to think about it is that if you can create new money for free, then you can buy anything you want at any time. If you can buy stuff with free money, while everyone else has to work for money, you will obviously be able to buy more stuff than everyone else. Over time, this free money lets you transfer more stuff from everyone else to yourself than you would have been able to get if you had to work for the money. This is the main reason that virtually all governments inflate the money supply. It lets them spend money that they have not earned, which lets them buy stuff without needing to produce anything. When they consume without producing, they are transferring resources from productive people to themselves. In this way, inflation acts a lot like a "tax". But it is a hidden tax that is difficult to see happening.

The new money also affects more people than just the government itself. When the money is first created, maybe a loaf of bread costs only $3. A year later, the same loaf of bread costs $3.30 because of all the new money circulating around and bidding up the prices. But that bidding up takes time. When the government first spends the new money, the bread is $3. A month later, the money has flowed from the government to the businesses that are closest to the government and now the price of bread is $3.10 because a few people are starting to bid more for bread. A year later, the money has flowed through the economy to the average citizen, everybody is bidding more, and now the price of bread is $3.30.

The government gets to spend the new money when it is worth the most bread. The businesses closest to the government get to spend the new money when it is worth slightly less. But the average citizen doesn't get to spend it until the full price increase has already taken effect. They have been buying bread at $3.30 for months before they ever see their wages go up. The end result is that the income of government contractors goes up *before* the prices of the things they buy goes up. But the wages of the average citizens are some of the last "prices" in the economy to get an increase. The wages of the average citizen only go up *after* the prices of the things they buy, which means they end up losing out. In this way, inflation benefits those businesses that have contracts with the government because they are the earliest recipients of the new money. This helps the government give preferential treatment to the businesses it works with most closely. This preferential treatment helps the government to secure support from those businesses when they are running for election and trying to get votes. It's the little people who get screwed.

## The Boom-Bust Cycle

It is clear why governments are so keen on inflating the money supply. In the short term, it lets them buy all the stuff they want without having to produce anything. But what about the longer term effects on the society? What happens in the economy when the money supply gets inflated?

Well, the extra supply of new money generally causes interest rates to be lower. Lenders (e.g. banks) compete for the business of borrowers (e.g. property developers, entrepreneurs, mortgage holders) by offering the borrowers lower interest rates. When there is more money available for lending, there is more competition among the lenders, which drives down the interest rate.

When interest rates are lower, people invest in more expensive, long-term projects, like building a skyscraper. The investors' hope is that they will be able to make more profit in the long term by building the bigger projects. The lower interest rates are what enables them to afford the large outlay for such a project.

Now, if the money available for lending had gone up because more people in the economy were *saving* their money and looking to invest in new projects, that would be all well and good. That would be a natural change in the interest rate. Interest rates would be going down because saving was going up. But when the government artificially introduces new money, they create an illusion. The artificially low interest rates make it look as though more people are saving and investing rather than consuming resources. But in fact, they are consuming just as many resources as before.

This means that the price of borrowed money (the interest rate) does not reflect the real balance between consumption and investment that is taking place in the economy. More resources are being consumed than the interest rate seems to indicate. The result is that there are actually not enough real resources available to complete all of the projects that got started in response to the lower interest rates.

This is the root cause of the repeated boom-bust cycles that we see in the economy. When the new money is created and interest rates are driven down, business people start investing in new large projects, which creates a perceived economic "boom". There are plenty of jobs available and things seem to be going well. But over time it becomes apparent that there are not enough resources to finish all the projects. The price of the real resources needed to complete these projects goes up in response to increased demand, the projects start going over budget and business ventures begin to fail. This economic "crash" is painful for many people, but it is actually healthy. The crash is really the mechanism by which the society re-establishes a proper balance between saving, consumption, prices and interest rates.

This boom-bust cycle is predictable. It happens whenever the government artificially introduces new money and drives down interest rates. It has many harmful effects. The crash phase can be especially difficult on families. It disrupts many people's lives when resources are reallocated and they are forced to change jobs or spend a period of time unemployed.

What is often most harmful about the bust phase is that it motivates the government to try and create a new boom. Because the bust phase is painful, a government that presides over the bust phase is in serious danger of losing public support. When people lose their jobs and feel poor, they are likely to be upset with whoever is running the show. To avoid this scenario, the government will often print a bunch more money to try and push the economy into a new and bigger boom phase than the one that triggered the bust. This is like drinking more alcohol to cure a hangover. When they keep creating bigger and bigger booms, they are just postponing the bigger and bigger bust that must eventually come. This is one reason why the rate at which governments inflate the money supply tends to accelerate over time.

## Potential Collapse of the Currency

If a currency gets inflated too much then people will eventually give up and stop using it. This is called a "hyperinflation" event. This is what happens when the new money is created so quickly that people refuse to hold onto it. They feel like the money is losing purchasing power so quickly that they immediately buy whatever real "stuff" they can find. They may not get a great deal, but it's better than waiting until tomorrow or next week and getting even less. This has happened with many currencies over the years. Examples in recent memory include Venezuela, Zimbabwe and Weimar Germany.

At this point we need to be cautious. Many people who are advocates of gold, silver or cryptocurrency have claimed that all fiat currencies inevitably experience a hyperinflation and collapse. That is not necessarily the case.

In theory, there is no reason why a government could not issue a fiat currency, but also restrain the rate at which they inflate that currency. If they kept the inflation rate fairly low, the money would likely never lose purchasing power fast *enough* for people to bother abandoning it.

Remember what we said earlier. New monetary standards get adopted because they are more convenient than the previous standard. Fiat money has been adopted over commodities like gold and silver because it is extremely convenient to use in daily transactions. With that convenience comes the risk that the government may rapidly inflate the money supply. But if the rate of inflation is low, most people will be willing to accept that inflation rather than give up the convenience of using the fiat money. It is only when the inflation rate gets extremely high that most people will choose to give up that convenience and start trading in non-fiat commodities.

History has shown us empirically that a society *can* function for an extended period of time on a currency where everybody knows (a) that the currency is being gradually inflated; and (b) that the currency is not redeemable for anything else. Everyone over about 25 years old has had plenty of opportunity to experience gradual inflation. They can see the cost of goods and services going up each year. They also know that the money is not redeemable for gold, silver or anything else. This has not caused people to abandon the currency. People with substantial wealth do not use the currency for long term saving. They save their wealth in assets like real-estate, company stocks and commodities (even gold and silver). But they still happily keep a bank account containing some of the gradually inflating currency which they use for daily transactions. The amount of purchasing power they lose to inflation is small enough that it is easier to just live with it than it is to abandon the convenience and the "network effect" of the existing currency. Why does this matter? Some advocates of gold and silver argue that cryptocurrency is just as prone to collapse as fiat money, because cryptocurrency and fiat money are both not "backed" by any other commodity. But experience shows us that this commodity "backing" is not actually necessary so long as the inflation rate of the fiat money remains low enough and the fiat money is very convenient to use. That high level of convenience is what incentivises people *not* to abandon the currency.

While a collapse in a fiat currency is certainly possible, it is *not* absolutely inevitable. The convenience factor can keep people using a fiat currency for a surprisingly long time, even in the face of huge declines in purchasing power. This is especially true if the government producing the currency creates artificial convenience factors, such as threatening to arrest anyone caught doing business in a currency other than the one they are printing. There is of course a breaking point. If the inflation gets bad enough, then no threats by the government can save it. After all, the police can't be everywhere and people need some way to effectively do business and feed their families. But that breaking point may be a lot further off than the advocates of "sound money" imagine it to be.

# Japan: A Case Study in the Extent of Inflation

To see how much inflation a currency can survive without being discarded, we should consider the case of Japan. Many people do not realise this, but at one time, one Japanese yen was basically the same type of coin as one US dollar. At the end of the 1800s, a one yen coin (from the Meiji era) had a weight of 26.96 grams and was composed 90% pure silver. At that same time, a one dollar coin (a "Morgan Dollar" in the picture below) had a weight of 26.73 grams and was also composed of 90% pure silver. The difference in weight was small enough that they had basically the same silver content. In broad strokes, it if fair to say that one yen was equivalent to one dollar.

Meiji Yen Coin

Morgan Dollar Coin

Fast forward to today and one US dollar can buy over 100 Japanese yen.

Now here's the crazy part. How much does 24.12 grams of silver cost today in US dollars? It used to cost $1 (when a one dollar coin *contained* 24.12 grams of silver). But today that amount of silver costs around $22. That seems like a big change. Your dollar today can only buy a little less than 5% as much silver as it could buy 100 years ago. Where did the other 95% of the purchasing power go? It went to the government through the "inflation tax". But if you think that's bad, then look at the yen. Today, the same 24.12 grams of silver that used to cost one yen now costs about 1,933 yen. That means that your yen today can only buy about 0.05% as much silver as it did back then. The Japanese government has successfully sneaked away 99.95% of the yen's purchasing power over that same time period.

What's the lesson here? The lesson is, don't assume that the US dollar is going to go away, even if it starts losing purchasing power at a rate much faster than it is losing purchasing power today. The Japanese yen has lost 100 times as much purchasing power over the past century as the US dollar has lost. But you know what? The yen is *still* the dominant currency in Japan.

# How Is Inflation Carried Out?

Governments have found many creative ways to inflate the money supply and transfer purchasing power from the citizens to themselves. The exact mechanism by which they achieve this goal has varied depending on what type of money was in use. It is important to understand this because people often think of cryptocurrency as being a protection against inflation. In reality, it is quite possible that governments will be able to re-use some of their old tricks to cause inflation in the future, even if we are using cryptocurrencies.

## Debasing the Coinage

In the days when gold and silver were minted into coins and exchanged directly, governments would inflate the supply by mixing the gold and silver with cheaper metals. In the Roman empire, successive emperors reduced the amount of silver that was in a standard "denarius" coin. Over the course of about 200 years, the coins went from being 90% silver to being only about 5% silver. By the end, they were basically just bronze coins with a thin coating of silver over them. Sounds pretty familiar right? Sounds a lot like the silver dollars and silver yen that likewise lost more than 95% of their purchasing power once they became paper dollars and paper yen. The impact of all this inflation was devastating for Rome's economy.

## Fractional Reserves

If you were worried about receiving an impure coin (like those created by the Roman emperors), one way around that would be to let professionals handle the actual metal. You could leave the gold and silver in a vault, staffed by experts who are good at testing coins and spotting fakes. But this strategy opens up a new vulnerability. If people conduct their exchanges using paper claims on the gold and silver in a vault somewhere, then the actual metal rarely gets moved out of the vault. Knowing this, the people running the vault can start handing out paper claims for more gold and silver than they actually have available. Let's say they have 1,000 real coins in storage and 1,000 paper notes that represent those coins. They notice that, in a given year, only about 50 coins ever get withdrawn at one time. Those 50 coins circulate around and usually get deposited back in the vault again. So they have 1,000 paper notes in circulation, but only 50 coins ever really get taken out. That's a ratio of one coin to every 20 notes. They figure that if the ratio holds, they should be able to issue 20,000 notes without needing any extra coins. At a ratio of 1:20, they only need to be able to produce 1,000 coins to back up those 20,000 notes. The rest of the notes will circulate without anyone actually trying to withdraw the gold or silver that they *think* the note represents.

When banks operate this way, it is called "fractional reserve banking". The bank guarantees that anyone can come in at any time and redeem the bank's notes for something tangible, such as a fixed amount of gold and silver. But the bank does not actually have enough gold and silver in the vault to honour that guarantee. If *everyone* tries to bring in their notes all at once, there won't be enough metal to go around. They only have a "fraction" of the required gold and silver sitting in reserve.

This is a form of fraud committed against the people who receive the notes. In effect, the bank is making promises that are impossible to keep. They promise to redeem the notes for gold and silver, which is why people use the notes as money and regard them as valuable. But the bank cannot actually redeem all the notes. The only way they can get away with this is that no one knows which notes are possible to redeem and which ones are not. When people try to redeem a note, it seems to work, as long as only a few people try to do it at once. Meanwhile, the bankers get to lend out all those extra notes and collect interest on them, even though they never had the metal to back them up.

What happens if a large number of people try to get their gold and silver out all at once? What happens when the bank can't redeem all of their claims? This is called a "bank run". Bankers who operate with fractional reserves live in fear of a bank run. If the bank had *full* reserves, then a bank run would be impossible, because they would always be able to honour all of their paper notes. In a society with consistent rule of law, a bank that was exposed for issuing paper notes with no backing would be charged with a crime. They would be prosecuted for fraud and forced to pay off their debt to the holders of their fake notes.

Unfortunately, we do not live in that world. Historically, banks have generally had a cozy relationship with governments. Sometimes they are actually one organisation (a "nationalised" bank), but other times they just scratch each other's backs. The bank helps the government to inflate the money supply. This lets the government spend the money on fighting wars, conquering new territory and campaigning for votes. In return, if the bank is ever in danger of experiencing a bank run, the government will typically pass a law that removes the bank's responsibility to redeem their paper notes.

In effect, the government will tell the citizens, "we know that the bank has issued notes under the promise to redeem them for gold and silver, but we have passed a law that lets them break that promise without any penalty."

Obviously banks and governments don't say this openly and directly. They say that they are letting the bank "suspend specie payment". They might even claim that it is only for a "limited time" or that it is necessary to keep the whole economy from collapsing. But the truth is that they are just giving a few favoured businesses (the banks) the special privilege of being able to demand that their loans are repaid while not having to repay their own debts to their customers.

This process of the government allowing banks to suspend gold and silver redemption has happened repeatedly in the United States (while the United States was still on a gold standard). Basically any time there was a recession or a danger of a bank run[2].

After World War II, in an attempt to stabilise exchange rates between different currencies, major countries all entered into the "Bretton Woods" agreement. Under this arrangement, all the different

______________

2   Rothbard, *History of Money and Banking in the United States*, 240.

currencies were pegged at fixed rates to the US dollar. The US dollar itself was pegged to gold at $35 per ounce. In theory, this meant that all the world's currencies were indirectly tied to gold through the US dollar. However, predictably, governments around the world inflated their own currencies by only keeping fractional reserves of US dollars. The US in turn inflated the dollar by only keeping fractional reserves of gold.

In the early 1970s, it became obvious that the US could not possibly honour all of its gold obligations at the rate of $35/ounce. There was not nearly enough gold in the US vaults to cover the dollars in circulation. President Nixon declared the complete break down of the gold redemption agreement when he ended the US dollar's convertibility to gold. Now, the world's currencies may have been pegged to the US dollar, but the US dollar itself was pegged to nothing. We had entered the world of *fiat* money.

## The Wild World of Fiat Inflation

The word "fiat" is Latin for "let it be done". When we talk about "fiat money", we are talking about "because I said so" money. Why is a $20 bill worth twice as much as a $10 bill? Because the government says so. That's all. They are both just bits of paper and ink.

Under a fiat money system, the government and the banks have no obligation to redeem the paper money for anything else. Not gold, not silver, not rice, not sand, nothing.

So what techniques does a government use to inflate the money supply when they are operating under a fiat system? The answer turns out to be shockingly complicated. Intuitively, we might assume that a pure fiat money system would mean that inflating the currency would be simple. Just press a few buttons and add some extra digits to the government's electronic bank account.

But in practice, the market naturally places some powerful restrictions on the amount of inflation that the government can get away with. Imagine that the government decided to increase the supply of money by 100x over the course of a year. People would quickly realise that the money was losing purchasing power at high speed and hyperinflation would set in. People would abandon the currency, the economy would slow down dramatically as people reverted to bartering and quality of life would plummet. That kind of thing goes over very badly with voters. So, at a minimum, the government wants to keep inflation low *enough* that the population doesn't turn against them or abandon the currency.

The government also needs to keep the public from asking too many awkward questions. They need to keep the monetary system very complex and mysterious so that the effects of inflation are less obvious to the average person. If someone complains that the government is "printing money" and decreasing the value of everyone's savings, having a very complex system makes it easier to dismiss that person as a crazy windbag. The government can say that they are not really "printing money", they are actually just:

- "stimulating demand in the economy"

- "lowering interest rates"

- "controlling the yield curve"

- "performing an asset swap"

- "providing liquidity"

There are plenty of euphemisms and misleading labels they can come up with. They can do this because they don't "create money" directly. They do it indirectly through interactions with the commercial banking system and through buying and selling debt instruments. A detailed description of that system is beyond the scope of this book[3]. Suffice to say, there's a

---

3   If you want a detailed account of how this system
    works, I recommend reading Bob Murhpy's

lot of smoke and mirrors involved. For now, here's an easy way to see the complexity of the fiat money-creation system. Ask an economist the question, "how much money is currently circulating in the economy?" They won't be able to give you a single, straight answer. They will immediately ask you follow up questions like these:

- Do consumer bank deposits count?

- Do bank reserves count?

- Do dollar-denominated money substitutes count?

They have to ask these questions because "money" in the fiat system gets shuffled through many different forms. Economists then disagree over which forms should be considered a part of the "money supply" in different contexts. Obviously, if we were using something like gold or silver as money, the answer would be simple. How much money is there? However many ounces of the physical metal are available. It's only with fiat money that the answer can become so complicated.

Another important point is that it is also possible for the money supply to *shrink* in the fiat money system.

_______________

"Understanding Money Mechanics" series, available at https://mises.org

This would be "deflation" rather than "inflation". Such deflation would tend to cause a decrease in consumer prices and a corresponding increase in the purchasing power of the money held by the public. One way this can happen is if many people start trying to reduce their level of debt. Since the fiat money supply is based on debt, a net-decrease in the amount of debt held in the society does lead to a decrease in the money supply. When this happens, it can help trigger the change from "boom" period to "bust" period in the business cycle that we discussed earlier. This goes to show how unstable the fiat money system can be.

## Conclusion: The Incentive to Inflate

Because the fiat money system is so complicated, economists and commentators disagree about how to calculate the total money supply. They even disagree over whether we are likely to experience inflation or deflation in the near-term future. But over the medium-to-long term the answer should be obvious.

Inflation is when the government artificially creates new money and adds it to the economy. The effect of this process is to transfer purchasing power from the public into the hands of the government. With that transfer of purchasing power also comes a transfer of wealth and political power.

While it is certainly possible for the money supply in the fiat system to shrink and experience a temporary deflation, the government always has a much stronger *incentive* to inflate the money supply than to deflate it. When they are creating money through inflation, they are transferring wealth and power to themselves. The people who have the most control over the money supply have nothing to gain by deflating and everything to gain by inflating. So over the long term, even if there are brief deflationary hiccups along the way, politicians and bankers can be counted on to keep the trend of inflation going, to keep transferring wealth and power to themselves and to keep gradually fleecing the public.

## Bitcoin: A New Hope

All of that history gives us the background that we need in order to understand Bitcoin. Bitcoin appeared on the scene in 2009, flowing out of the 2008 housing crisis in the USA and the accompanying global financial crisis. Bitcoin was a new currency, built for the Internet, based on a simple but radical innovation in computer science.

The creator of Bitcoin explicitly positioned it as a competitor to the existing banking and monetary system. The very first "block" in the Bitcoin blockchain contained an embedded message reproducing a newspaper headline:

> The Times 03/Jan/2009 Chancellor on brink of second bailout for banks

This message served two purposes. The first was to prove that the block had been created no earlier than 03-Jan-2009 when the newspaper headline was released. The second was to position Bitcoin as a solution to a timely political problem: bank bailouts. The central banks of various countries were printing money in order to keep commercial banks from going bankrupt. The commercial banks had gotten into trouble by lending money to lots of people who were not able to pay it back. These debts were not going to be repaid and were considered "toxic assets" by the banks. That is, they were assets that were not actually worth as much as the bank had expected. To get the commercial banks out of trouble, the central bank had printed a lot of new money to buy these toxic assets from the commercial banks and "bail them out". This effectively meant that the central banks were stealing purchasing power from the general public in order to protect the fortunes of their friends in the commercial banking system.

Under the established banking system, the public was helpless to do anything about this. They could only watch as their purchasing power was snatched away. But with Bitcoin, there was the promise of something different. Bitcoin was a new form of digital money that had a limited supply and could not be created at will by any central authority (like a central bank). Bitcoin had the potential to end this power imbalance in society once and for all. Your money would be your money. No one would be able to snatch it away or devalue it by printing more for themselves.

So, how is this possible? If Bitcoin is just digital data in computers, how can the supply be limited? Computer data can be copied so easily. Can't I just make duplicate copies of my "coins" and increase the supply? Many people (including myself!) thought that this problem was unsolvable. That is, until the Bitcoin technical paper was released and proved us wrong.

## The Technology in a Nutshell

A primary goal of this book is that if you decide to invest in cryptocurrency, you will *really understand* what it is that you are buying. That does not necessarily mean that you need to understand all the nerdy cryptography, math and computer science concepts[4]. What you really need to know is: what does it do and is it really secure?

The fundamental innovation that powers Bitcoin is called a "proof-of-work blockchain"[5]. A blockchain is just a convenient way of structuring data in chronological order. In the case of Bitcoin, the data is a ledger of transactions. Since the blockchain gives us a chronological record of transactions, we can use that record to reconstruct the balance in each account.

---

4    I have a background in computer science myself, so I personally felt compelled to understand cryptocurrency at a technical level before ever trying it. But it is not realistic to expect that from everyone. If you do want to understand the technical details then the best place to start is with the original Bitcoin whitepaper, available at https://bitcoin.com/bitcoin.pdf

5    This book is about the larger world of cryptocurrency, not just Bitcoin. Bitcoin is a blockchain based on proof-of-work. Not all cryptocurrencies use a block "chain" and not all of them use the proof-of-work as a consensus mechanism. But Bitcoin was the first and simplest implementation of a cryptocurrency. To understand the innovations that came later, you must understand what they are trying to improve upon.

Having a ledger is nice, but we could already do that with a spreadsheet or a conventional database. The real genius of Bitcoin was taking that ledger and attaching it to a proof-of-work system. The proof-of-work system allows the Bitcoin network to solve something called the "double-spend problem". Let's say that I have 10 "coins" assigned to me in the ledger. I set up two computers with a timer so that both computers will try to send a transaction at exactly the same time. One computer is in Canada and it will try to send 10 coins to my friend Alice. The other computer is in Australia and it will try to send *those same* 10 coins to my friend Bob. Now, only one of these transactions can succeed. I only have 10 coins to give, not 20, so Alice and Bob can't *both* receive 10 coins, otherwise I would be creating new money in the system (inflation!). One of these transactions must succeed and the other must fail. I cannot be allowed to "double-spend" these coins.

In the legacy banking system the double-spend problem is solved by having some authority figure decide which transaction succeeds, i.e. the bank. The problem with that system is that the bank gets to dictate everything. They can freeze my account, they can refuse to send money to a particular friend of mine, etc.

The proof-of-work system gives us a way to solve the double-spend problem without relying on a central authority to decide which transaction succeeds and which one fails. Suppose I do the experiment above and broadcast my transaction to Alice in Canada at the same time that I broadcast a conflicting transaction to Bob in Australia. All the Bitcoin users in Canada will probably see the transaction to Alice first, while the Bitcoin users in Australia will see the transaction to Bob first. This is because Internet communications take slightly longer to reach the other side of the globe than they take to reach the next town. If we can't agree on the the timing of which transaction came first, then how can all of the Bitcoin users around the world come to an agreement about which transaction should be accepted and which should be rejected?

This is what proof-of-work does. The proof-of-work system allows anyone in the world to download 10 conflicting copies of the ledger and still be able to know for certain which copy is "correct". Each copy of the ledger has a different amount of "work" attached to it. That work represents the amount of computing power across the network that is "voting" for that version of the ledger. If you can see all the different versions, you can clearly see which one is being chosen and agreed upon by everyone else.

By connecting proof-of-work to the blockchain ledger, the Bitcoin system allows all the participants to come to consensus about who owns each coin without anyone being "in charge" of anyone else.

## Can it be Hacked?

This is always a tough question for people who are rightly cautious of anything involving computers. If Bitcoin is run on computers, and computers can be hacked, then can Bitcoin also be hacked?

The short answer is no, Bitcoin cannot be hacked.

Individual computer systems can be hacked. But Bitcoin is *not* an individual computer system. Bitcoin is a method by which *many* computer systems come to consensus about transaction information. Asking "can Bitcoin be hacked" misunderstands the type of problem that Bitcoin solves. In a sense, the Bitcoin network assumes that every participant is trying to break the rules and steal from every other participant at all times. In an environment where we assume that everyone is trying to steal from each other already, what does it even mean to "hack" the system? If someone tries to break the rules and steal funds, they are doing exactly what the system expects. Bitcoin is purpose-built for handling exactly that situation. If you hack a particular computer running the Bitcoin software and change the encoded rules, you are just going to force that *individual* computer out of the consensus with the rest of the network. But the rest of the network will still be in consensus with each other and the system will continue merrily on its way.

Now, that is not to say that there are no dangers from computer hackers. You probably use online banking right now for fiat currency. If a hacker managed to break into your computer and install a key logger, they could use that to find out your banking password, log into your bank account and move your money. If that happened, we would say that they had hacked *your* computer. But we would not say that they have "hacked the dollar". Likewise, if a hacker managed to break into your computer and get your Bitcoin private keys, they would be able to take your money. But that would be because they hacked into *your* computer, not because they had fundamentally broken the Bitcoin network.

## How Secure is the Cryptography Technology?

The Bitcoin network itself (and cryptocurrency in general) is based on two of the most battle-tested cryptography methods of all time. The first is called public-key cryptography. Every website that uses "https" to encrypt data (instead of unencrypted "http") is using public-key cryptography. If that gets broken, every bank website fails and the whole financial system fails with it. How much effort do you think has been spent by researchers and hackers on trying to break that? A mind-blowing amount of effort over many decades. But it's still standing strong.

The other technique is called a "one-way hash algorithm". These are used by virtually every website on the Internet that requires a password. Again, if you found a way to break this cryptographic technique, you would potentially be able to log into any account on any website in the world. Computer science departments at universities around the world have been working on breaking this technique non-stop for decades. The math has proven to be rock solid.

Like I said, these are battle-tested cryptographic principles. You already trust them with your critical data every day without realising it. Cryptocurrency doesn't require any new leaps of faith in this area.

# The Economic Advantages of a Cryptocurrency

Why would we want a cryptocurrency? What advantages does it give us over commodity money (like gold and silver) or fiat money (like the US dollar)? At the start of this book I outlined the key properties that made gold and silver attractive as a medium of exchange. Gold and silver are: recognisable, portable, divisible, fungible, durable and scarce.

Cryptocurrency has strengths over gold and silver in some areas and weaknesses in others.

## Clear Strengths

- **Recognisable:** verifying that you have not received counterfeit cryptocurrency is very fast and easy compared to gold and silver. There are a variety of ways to counterfeit precious metals, mostly involving mixing in cheaper metals and leaving only a thin coating of the real thing. Counterfeiters can be extremely sophisticated, producing coins and bars in very official-looking packaging copied from well known mints. Verifying the purity of gold or silver bullion is a complicated business.  You can do it by precisely measuring the weight, size and electrical conductivity of the sample. These days most dealers do it by using a \$20,000 XRF (X-ray fluorescence) machine to detect the proportions of chemical elements in a coin or bar. This all requires expertise, training and equipment[6]. By contrast, a cryptocurrency transaction can be authenticated and verified in a fraction of a second by any smartphone.

- **Portable:** Cryptocurrency, being entirely digital, is the most portable money ever created. Obviously cryptocurrency is cheaper and easier to move around than gold and silver. But it is actually even cheaper and easier to move than fiat money. Fiat transfers mean that either physical notes must be transported or else a labyrinth of international banking regulations must be navigated. Cryptocurrency is inherently "borderless" and can be transferred from one person to another over any distance without extra cost.

---

6   For this reason, if you are going to buy some gold or silver bullion then it is best to buy it from a professional dealer whom you trust. They will have the expertise to spot a fake and they will be motivated to protect the reputation of their business by checking carefully for counterfeits.

- **Divisible:** cryptocurrency is more readily divisible than gold and silver. While gold and silver can be melted down and split into very small denominations, there is a physical limit to how small the coins can be while remaining usable. It also requires time, labour and equipment to break apart and recombine gold and silver into different weights. Cryptocurrency can be divided down to any level of precision and recombined with essentially zero effort.

- **Scarcity:** cryptocurrencies typically have an embedded emission schedule, where coins are created at a very slow and predictable rate. This means that they are even more resistant to sudden increases in the supply than gold and silver (where supply could be increased quickly if a new mine were discovered or a new technology were invented for extracting the metal from the ground).

## Potential Weaknesses

- **Fungible:** any ounce of gold ultimately has the same value as any other ounce. They are generally interchangeable (that is to say, fungible). If a stash of gold jewellery gets melted down and turned into coins, there is no way to tell that the gold in the coins used to be in jewellery form. Likewise, individual silver coins (assuming they are the same shape, weight and purity) are not distinguishable from one another in any meaningful sense. This is not *necessarily* the case with a cryptocurrency. The nature of most cryptocurrencies is that there is a publicly visible record of the payments done within the network. There are no real world identities directly attached to those payments, but there is a certain amount of information that can be gleaned. That means that if you accept a payment in cryptocurrency, there is a chance that you are accepting money that was used for something illegal last week (without your knowledge). If a detective traces the funds from that illegal activity, you may become a person of interest in that case, even though it is actually nothing to do with you. Different cryptocurrencies have very different characteristics when it comes to privacy and fungibility. Some are extremely private and fungible while others are quite transparent. We will say more about this in a later chapter.

- **Durable:** Gold and silver have been functioning as money for millennia. There is every reason to think that they will continue to be valued by people around the world for a long time to come. Cryptocurrency is different. It is a very new invention in world history. The first cryptocurrency, Bitcoin, is only a decade old. Additionally, the Bitcoin from 2009 is not the same as the Bitcoin of today. Improvements have been made to the software, new tools have been created to increase its utility and the hardware used to run it has changed dramatically. When Bitcoin was first created, it was mined using desktop computers. Today it is mined using gigantic server farms full of custom-designed computer chips that do nothing but generate block hashes. What will Bitcoin look like in 10 years? What about 100 years? What will have changed in the technology landscape as a whole? It is very difficult to know the answers to these questions. There is a lot of potential for growth there, but there is also a risk that something else will come along with superior technology and a better user experience, which will supersede Bitcoin as the dominant cryptocurrency. It's not crazy to buy gold bars and expect to hold them in a vault for 50 years without ever needing to touch them. It is unrealistic to think that you will buy a cryptocurrency today and the network running that cryptocurrency will remain totally unchanged over even 10 years, let alone 50. The changes may actually be very good. But they represent "unknowns", which may be a concern for the conservative investor.

## Predetermined Monetary Policy

What about in relation to fiat money? Why would we use a cryptocurrency rather than the US dollar or the Japanese yen? One critical reason is because cryptocurrency has a predetermined "monetary policy". You can know with certainty exactly how many units of a cryptocurrency exist today and how many will exist in the future. The whole point of fiat currencies is that the government can create new money whenever they like rather than committing themselves to a particular supply level in advance.

This ability to create new money is what allows the government to inflate the money supply and steal purchasing power away from ordinary people.

Different cryptocurrencies have a variety of different monetary policies. Bitcoin famously has a "supply cap" of 21 million. This is such a central part of

Bitcoin's brand that different forks of Bitcoin have generally kept this policy in place. But not all cryptocurrencies have an absolute supply cap. Monero does not have an absolute maximum supply. Instead it has a fixed (very low) emission rate. New Monero coins will continue to be created and given to Monero miners forever, but the rate at which that these new coins are created will continually decrease *as a percentage* of the existing supply, so that the inflation rate asymptotically *approaches* zero.

There are advantages to both strategies. On the one hand, the Bitcoin strategy of a final supply cap is very easy to understand and it has been a powerful part of the sales pitch for Bitcoin that "only 21 million will ever be created". On the other hand, when the cap is reached, miners will no longer receive any fixed reward for securing the network. They will only receive the fees paid by people wishing to transact. Currently, the "block rewards" (the newly created quantities of Bitcoin) make up the vast majority of the miners' profits. The economics of Bitcoin may change for the worse in an environment where miners are primarily rewarded with transaction fees rather than newly minted coins. Miners may be incentivised to game the system to try and increase fees for the users. Monero avoids this problem by maintaining at least a small fixed reward for miners to maintain the network in perpetuity.

There are many other nuanced differences of monetary policy between different cryptocurrencies. Should the decreasing emission rate be a smooth curve (Monero) or be subject to periodic "halvings" (Bitcoin)? Should the time frame for reaching the final supply cap be measured in decades (Bitcoin), or in months (Nano)? Should new coins be emitted only to miners (Bitcoin, Bitcoin Cash, Monero), or should coins also be emitted to the software developers (Firo, eCash), to network service providers (Dash) or to some other entities in the ecosystem?

There is no single "correct" answer to these questions. Different people will see the strengths and weaknesses differently. But what we find in the world of cryptocurrency is a *free market* in monetary policy. Rather than being forced to accept the government creating new money in their own accounts at will, we can instead choose to opt-in to whichever monetary policy we think is the best by using a cryptocurrency that is based upon that policy.

## Resistance to Government Tyranny

The other critical advantage of cryptocurrency over fiat and commodity money is its resistance to interference by governments. The "crypto" part of the word "cryptocurrency" means that the mechanism for transferring funds is based on battle-tested cryptography and mathematics. If you hold cryptocurrency, you can be confident that the only person who can authorise a transaction is the person who holds the private key. This is the origin of the important catch phrase "not your keys, not your coins".

This creates "confiscation resistance". There is no law that a government can pass that will enable them to generate a transaction and make it look like you authorised it. If they don't have your private key, it simply cannot be done. A private key is also a very easy thing to store and keep safe. Most cryptocurrencies use the dictionary method for representing private keys for easy storage. A private key normally looks like a long string of random characters. But using some clever techniques, you can represent the same information as a set of words from a known dictionary. A standard Bitcoin "seed phrase" consists of only 12 words. You can write those 12 words on a piece of paper, hide that piece of paper somewhere and that is all the information you need in order to recover your funds. If you're worried about someone finding the piece of paper, you can simply memorise the 12 words in your brain.

You can get on a plane and fly across international borders with nothing but those 12 words in your memory and your money will effectively come with you. There is no cash and no gold coins in your bag for anyone to find. If you're worried about a written-down seed phrase being destroyed in a fire, you can engrave it on a piece of metal and store it in a locked safe. Because a simple 12-word phrase is so small and portable, the possibilities for securing it are nearly endless. The right method for your particular case simply depends on what type of threats you expect to encounter.

That is not to say that there are no threats at all from a tyrannical government. Given that they cannot fake a transaction authorisation, what can they do? Well, in order for a transaction to be processed, the network of computers around that cryptocurrency needs to come to consensus that a transaction is valid and should be considered as settled. One thing that the government could do is to threaten violence against any network participants who dared to participate in processing a transaction from someone the government doesn't like. The government could produce a blacklist of cryptocurrency addresses that should not be allowed to transact. Node operators would be compelled to mark any transactions from those addresses as "invalid" even if they were signed by the correct private key. If node operators did not adopt that blacklist and mark those transactions as invalid, then they would be subject to fines, imprisonment, etc. In this way, the government could attempt to "freeze" a cryptocurrency account and censor the transactions of people it deemed to be bad actors.

However, because cryptocurrency networks are globally distributed, this strategy is very unlikely to be effective. For example, suppose that the government of China tries to compel Chinese Bitcoin miners to censor the accounts of Chinese political dissidents. Bitcoin miners across the rest of the world would still be able to process the transaction. If the Chinese miners kept refusing to recognise the valid transactions, eventually one of two things would happen. On the one hand, the Chinese miners may simply fade into irrelevance because they had fallen out of consensus with the rest of the network. On the other hand, there may be a sufficiently large portion of the network that would bend to the demands of the Chinese government that the network would "fork" and we would be left with two different versions of Bitcoin. One version would respect the Chinese government's blacklist, the other would not. People who owned Bitcoin before the split would now own two separate coins in two separate cryptocurrencies. We might call these two cryptocurrencies "Bitcoin Uncensored" and "Bitcoin China". These two distinct currencies would trade freely against one another. There would be an exchange rate between them set by the open market and we would quickly see which one was valued more highly by the public at large. In all likelihood, it would be Bitcoin Uncensored that would be most favoured because that is the one that refuses to let its users be censored by a tyrannical government.

This ability to "fork" the network when bad actors try to undermine it is a critical feature of the system. This is part of what gives cryptocurrencies the property of "censorship resistance". Even if a government tries to use threats of violence to censor transactions, people in less oppressed jurisdictions can simply fork away and ignore the threats made by governments in more oppressed areas of the world.

We have seen this play out in practice. Wikileaks was able to use Bitcoin to receive donations after its accounts at traditional banks were frozen. This is what kept their whole organisation from going bust. This proves that, when push comes to shove, cryptocurrency has been much more difficult to censor than fiat money. We have also seen in history that commodity money like gold can be confiscated by the government, largely because it tends to be stored in centralised vaults to economise on security costs rather than every single individual holding all of their own gold at home. The US government (under Franklin D. Roosevelt) ordered the seizure of all gold bullion and coins, forcing citizens to sell their gold to the government at well below the market rate. Gold ownership remained illegal in the United States until the 1970s. Laws allowing this type of gold seizure by the government also exist in other countries.

If they've done it once, they can do it again. If your gold is stored in a large vault when a currency crisis hits, the government may just decide that it is in the national interest for *your* gold to become *their* gold. In exchange, you will receive paper money that rapidly depreciates against the value of the gold that was taken from you. But cryptocurrency does not need to be stored in a vault to be secure. You don't need to secure physical coins or bars behind reinforced walls and complicated locks. All you need is to secure 12 words.

## The "Intrinsic Value" of a Cryptocurrency

Gold and silver have a wide variety of uses. Jewellery, consumer electronics, dentistry, solar panels, antimicrobial lab coats. All of these things use gold or silver. This has led many people to conclude that gold and silver have "intrinsic value". Whatever happens to gold and silver spot prices in the craziness of financial markets, gold and silver will always be worth *something* because they are so useful. There is not much danger that gold and silver bullion will ever go to $0.00 in price and be worth nothing.

Critics will point out that cryptocurrency is not used in manufacturing any products. On that basis, they will conclude that cryptocurrency has no "intrinsic value". On this view, there is nothing but hot air and gambling that is keeping the price of a cryptocurrency from going to $0.00 and the cryptocurrency holdings of speculators from being worth nothing at all.

This view is incorrect on several counts which must be clearly understood if we are to understand the role of cryptocurrency in the world today and in our own portfolios.

## Intrinsic Value Doesn't Exist

First we need to understand that there is no such thing as "intrinsic value". No commodity or product has value in and of itself. It is considered valuable by particular *people*. In a world with no people, a pile of diamonds would not be worth any more than a pile of sand. The only reason the diamonds have more value in our current world is that there are people who value them more than sand and people are willing to do work or trade other goods and services in order to obtain diamonds.

Gold and silver also do not have intrinsic value. People regard them as valuable because they have various uses. But suppose that tomorrow we discovered a new element on the periodic table that had all the desirable properties of gold but which was much more abundant. Suppose that we could mine it for a few cents per tonne. A few people might still use gold for jewellery out of tradition and nostalgia. But the industrial uses of gold would be gone. Everyone would use this new cheaper metal for most applications.

That would cause the price of gold to plummet. So the value of gold is not "intrinsic". It is not "within" the gold. The value always comes from what some other person is willing to pay for it. And what they are willing to pay for it depends on the benefit that they expect to get from it.

Now, it should be admitted that we are much more likely to invent a new cryptocurrency than we are to discover a new type of abundant, useful metal. New cryptocurrencies can always be created. If we are going to buy one that already exists, we need to have some reason for thinking that it is going to stick around and not just be replaced by a newer cryptocurrency that uses some kind of improved technology or algorithms. We will talk more about evaluating and selecting cryptocurrencies in a later chapter.

## Cryptocurrency *Does* Have Industrial Uses

As we noted above, gold and silver fans will often argue that cryptocurrency has no industrial use the way that gold and silver do. But this is not strictly true either. There *are* industrial uses for cryptocurrency.

The easiest way to illustrate this point is to consider the "alternative goods" that cryptocurrency networks can replace. When we transact using cryptocurrency, we suddenly find that we no longer need the services of Mastercard, VISA, PayPal or Stripe in order to do business. We can transact directly with anyone, anywhere in the world. We often pay surprisingly high fees to payment processing companies for their services in helping us transfer money quickly and securely. By using cryptocurrency, we get those same benefits for a much lower cost.

If people are willing to pay financial services companies for facilitating transactions, then whatever value they are getting is also value that can be found in a functioning cryptocurrency network.

But the only way to get those benefits from the cryptocurrency network is to use the cryptocurrency as your medium of exchange. You cannot use the Bitcoin network to move dollars or euros. You can only use it to move bitcoins. If you want to get the benefits of fast and secure transfers of funds, you have to hold a balance of bitcoins. In the same way that gold and silver's industrial uses put a "floor" under their price, the ability of cryptocurrency networks to facilitate commerce (especially online) also puts a floor under their price.

## Cryptocurrency: The Best of Both Worlds

Our own life experience tells us that fiat money can and does work very well for running an economy. Even though it cannot be used to produce any products the way that metals can, the dollar is a very efficient system for facilitating transactions. We can pay quickly and securely using banks to facilitate fiat money transactions. The only problem is that using fiat money locks us into a system where someone else has control of our financial freedom and where our purchasing power can be stolen by inflation.

Gold gives us the freedom of being able to control our own money and protect our purchasing power, but gold is difficult to use in transactions because it is relatively slow and expensive to move around. This is what leads people to start using paper fiat money in the first place.

Cryptocurrency gives us the best of both worlds. Cryptocurrency is money that cannot be inflated, that gives us the freedom to control our own money, *and also* is cheap and easy to move around. That's why it is such an exciting new development. Cryptocurrency is perhaps the most effective and efficient form of money ever discovered.

## Bitcoin's Big Flaw

At this stage, you are hopefully starting to see some of the great advantages that come from using cryptocurrency compared to other forms of money. But this is a book for conservative investors. We are not here looking to create hype. We want to examine the real-world issues that cryptocurrencies face.

For most people today, cryptocurrency is virtually synonymous with Bitcoin. Bitcoin was the very first cryptocurrency to genuinely solve the double-spend problem. It is an amazingly clever piece of technological innovation. But it is definitely not perfect.

Some people mistakenly believe that because Bitcoin is digital, everything about it must be instant and free of cost. Sending an email or a tweet is free and instant, so why should sending a Bitcoin transaction be any different?

While some Bitcoin transactions can be relatively fast and cheap, executing a Bitcoin transaction under the wrong circumstances can take many hours and can cost the equivalent of US $50 or more in transaction fees.

This is due to particular engineering trade-offs that exist in the Bitcoin network. Back around 2016-2017 a highly controversial decision was taken to artificially limit the maximum throughput of the Bitcoin network to around 5-7 transactions per second. The upside of this decision is that it is possible for low-end, consumer-grade computers to handle that amount of data without ever breaking a sweat. This makes it cheap enough for lots of people to fully validate every transaction in the Bitcoin network using their own home computer. The downside is that when the demand for "space" in the transaction queue exceeds 5-7 transactions per second, the only option is for wait times to increase and transaction fees to skyrocket as people bid against each other for earlier positions in the processing queue.

Of course, if Bitcoin was going to be used as a global form of money, 5-7 transactions per second is nowhere near enough to support the amount of economic activity that goes on every day. PayPal alone has been estimated to handle somewhere around 1,600 transactions per second. If Bitcoin cannot handle the capacity of PayPal, then there's no way it can replace global payment systems on an even larger scale like that of VISA or Mastercard.

## The Impact of a Throughput Cap on Monetary Properties

Ultimately, the decision to put an artificial cap on Bitcoin's throughput totally undermines most of the key advantages that Bitcoin had as an alternative form of money.

- **Portability:** it's much more expensive to move Bitcoin around than fiat.

- **Divisibility:** small amounts become unspendable because they are smaller than the transaction fees that it would cost to spend them.

- **Fungibility:** technologies for obscuring transaction history (which typically rely on doing multiple transactions) become prohibitively expensive.

When Bitcoin was first rising to fame and becoming popular, many large companies started to adopt it as a method of payment for their customers. These included tech giants like Microsoft and Valve. But as the usage of Bitcoin hit this artificial throughput cap, the user experience became terrible. The long wait times and high fees were so painful that many companies that had adopted Bitcoin for payments actually dropped it and went back to accepting only fiat money.

Clearly this situation was totally unworkable. Something had to be done if there was going to be any hope of cryptocurrency gaining wide adoption in society. Within the Bitcoin community, there were two basic strategies proposed for how to deal with this problem. One strategy was to remove the artificial throughput limit, to allow the Bitcoin network to process as many transactions as necessary, and tolerate the fact that higher-end, professional and server-grade computers would be required in order to run a node capable of validating all the transactions. In this strategy, the plan was to keep working at making the validation process more efficient so that the higher computing requirements would not get out of hand. However, the danger exists that if the network cannot be made efficient enough and the throughput keeps rising, the only entities with computers large enough to handle it may be governments and large corporations. In this case, the "centralisation" of the network nodes into fewer hands could enable the rich and powerful to take control of the network and impose their own rules upon the users.

The other strategy was to keep the throughput limit in place, commit to the lowest end computers always being able to validate everything, but tolerate long wait times and expensive fees in order for users to transact. In this strategy, the plan was to work on building a new type of transactional network to take some of the throughput pressure away from Bitcoin's main network.

Today, the original Bitcoin network has divided into two separate networks, each following one of these two strategies. One is called "Bitcoin Cash" (abbreviated BCH). This is the network that chose to remove the artificial throughput limit in order to keep transactions fast and cheap for everyone. The other is usually still just called "Bitcoin" (abbreviated BTC). This is the network that has kept the artificial throughput limit and begun work on a new network overlay that is better able to handle high transaction throughput. This new project is called the "Lightning Network" and it is hoped to be the technology that will enable Bitcoin to support fast and cheap payments again, like it did before the throughput cap was reached. With the addition of the Lightning Network, the BTC camp hopes to achieve the goal of fast, cheap transactions without ever sacrificing the ability of low-end computers to fully validate the base network.

At first glance, it might seem like the addition of the Lightning Network gives Bitcoin BTC the best of both worlds. But it turns out that the Lightning Network has some significant drawbacks of its own.

## The Lightning Network

The basic architecture of the Lightning Network is that two parties establish a "channel" between themselves and then send transactions back and forth. Transactions inside the channel are only seen by the people using that channel. They are not broadcast publicly and are usually not committed into the Bitcoin blockchain. A simple way to think of it is to imagine people putting cash into a lock box before a poker game. The players each put their cash in at the start of the night and the box is locked. They play poker all night by moving chips around the table instead of the actual cash.

At the end of the night all the chips are counted up. Then someone opens the lock box and distributes the cash in proportion to how many chips each person has accumulated during the poker game.

Instead of transacting with cash every time a hand of poker is played, players just transact with chips. They might do a hundred transactions over the course of the evening using those chips. But there is only one transaction done with cash at the end of the night.

In a similar way, when people open a lightning channel, they lock up their Bitcoin and exchange it for "chips" that can only be moved around inside their lightning channel. When someone wants to move funds out of the channel, both sides turn in their chips and receive the equivalent amount of Bitcoin back out of the "lock box". This allows many small transactions done in the lightning channel to be merged into one large transaction on the main Bitcoin network. Merging transactions this way is what allows the users to save on transaction fees.

While this is a very clever and interesting system, it leads to some truly difficult problems.

# Lightning Problems: Channel Management Costs

To open a lightning channel (to put money in the "lock box"), each person must do a normal transaction on the Bitcoin base network. This may not sound like a big deal, but it means that there is a significant cost to bringing each new person onto the network. It also means there is a hard limit to the speed at which people can be brought in. Since the base Bitcoin network has a hard throughput limit, and it requires a transaction to bring someone on, there is a limit on the number of people that can be brought onto the lightning network over any given period of time. Here's some back-of-the-napkin math.

- Maximum of 7 transactions per second.

- Attempting to add 1 billion people to the network for global adoption.

- 1 billion / 7 = number of seconds required to do one transaction per person.

- Number of seconds required = 142,857,143 seconds = about 4.5 years.

Imagine that the whole Bitcoin network was doing nothing but open new lightning channels (no moving coins between exchanges, no using the main network for payments, no *closing* lightning channels for security reasons). Even in that extreme case, it would still take 4.5 years to give 1 billion people the ability to receive funds via the lightning network. That's if those people were all ready for the onboarding process when it was their turn. In practice, the network is used for lots of different things, so even this timeline is far too optimistic. If only 10% of the network capacity is used for opening new channels to bring people in, then it would take 45 years to get a billion people initiated into the system. That's a long time to wait to be able to use a payment system! By contrast, other cryptocurrency networks have no hard limit on the rate at which they can add new users. In most other cryptocurrency networks, adding a new user with the ability to receive funds does not require a transaction and costs nothing.

## Lightning Problems: Routing Payments

Because lightning channels are only between specific parties, you cannot just send funds directly to anyone you like. There needs to be a series of intermediate channels existing between the sender and the receiver. If you have a channel connecting you to Alice, Alice has a channel to Bob and Bob has a channel to Charlie, *then* you can send funds to Charlie. But if you want to send 10 coins to Charlie and the channel between Bob and Charlie only has a total of 5 coins inside their shared "lock box" then you are out of luck. You have to keep trying different channel paths in the hopes of eventually finding one that has enough funds available in every intermediate channel. But if you can't find one, then the only way to pay Charlie is to add a new channel between you and Charlie directly. That means that you've wasted a bunch of time testing channel paths that have failed and now you also have to pay a high fee to open a channel to Charlie before you can send him the funds.

But the routing problem is even more complicated than it first appears. Every time a payment succeeds in the Lightning Network, it changes the balance of funds in each channel on the path that was used. If you try to map out the channel paths available for sending payments to a particular person, you have to continuously update your map because the funds available in those channels keep changing. This is an extraordinarily difficult computational problem that currently has no compelling solution at large scales. It appears that routing payments in the Lightning Network will always involve a degree of trial and error, which makes the payment process slower and less reliable.

## Lightning Problems: Incentives to Centralise

Ultimately, there is one easy solution to these sorts of user-experience problems with the Lightning Network. The easy solution is to drastically centralise the network. This can be done through creating apps and cloud services that handle all of the channel management issues for the user. But this is most effective if the user does not have direct custody of their own money. It is a step back into the world of fiat banking, where the bank really controls your money and can seize your assets or freeze your accounts at any time.

That's a huge problem because the whole rationale for creating the Lightning Network was so that the Bitcoin network could remain as *decentralised* as possible. That was the goal of the artificial throughput limit, to make it so that anyone and everyone could have a fast enough computer to handle the throughput and validate all the transactions.

If the Lightning Network can only work by becoming *centralised*, then it has failed in its mission to keep the overall system *decentralised*.

In the worst case, this centralisation could let governments or other bad actors take control of the system, freeze accounts, seize funds and even start inflating the supply again. It could ruin the whole mission of cryptocurrency.

## Conclusion

It should be clear by now that the issue of "scaling" in cryptocurrency is very complex. The split between the Bitcoin Cash (BCH) and Bitcoin+Lightning (BTC+LN) camps shows us that the correct engineering trade-offs are not obvious. Proponents of each strategy believe that theirs is best way to achieve the goal of having a decentralised monetary network that can reach global adoption. Both groups have reasons why they think the other camp's strategy will fail. Failure could come by becoming too centralised or by having a user experience that is too frustrating and difficult to achieve mass adoption. As investors and speculators, if we are going to hold part of our portfolio denominated in either BCH or BTC, it is up to us to investigate the issues and decide for ourselves whether we think either of them are actually capable of living up to the promises. Maybe one camp is capable of achieving mass adoption and decentralisation while the other is not. Maybe neither strategy is correct and the goal of a mass-adopted, decentralised monetary network can only be achieved by using a whole new architecture that is substantially different from either version of Bitcoin. Maybe one of the myriad of other cryptocurrency projects with their various tweaks and novel ideas is going to be the eventual winner. The rest of this book will introduce you to the types of questions that you need to ask in order to better anticipate which of the available types of "money" the market is most likely to adopt.

# The Future of Money

So far in this book we have been looking at the *past* history of money. We have seen how the world moved from commodity money (gold and silver) to fiat money (government-issued paper). We have seen how Bitcoin arrived on the scene and brought with it the potential for a new and improved form of money based on computers and cryptography.

But investing is ultimately about the future, not the past. To make a profit we need to take the lessons learned from looking at the past and use them to anticipate how the *future* of money is likely to play out.

As I see it, there are basically three types of "money" that are likely to play a significant role in our future. One is digital currencies issued by governments. Another is the ongoing role of precious metals as the world's longest-running money system. The final one, the one that interests us most as potential crypto investors, is the next generation of cryptocurrency. We have seen that the original Bitcoin system has engineering challenges to solve in order to reach global adoption. We need to figure out which projects are the most promising when it comes to meeting those challenges. Those are the ones worth speculating on.

## Central Bank Digital Currencies

You may have heard people talking about something called "Fedcoin". What they are referring to is a version of the US dollar that is purely digital and is issued directly by the Federal Reserve (which is the central bank of the USA).

Other countries are also making moves towards issuing digital currencies, notably China. These digital currencies are known as CBDCs (Central Bank Digital Currencies).

What's the difference between "Fedcoin" and the US dollar as it exists today? After all, we already move a lot of fiat money digitally. Most fiat money is not in the form of actual paper notes. Well, the big difference is that a CBDC would give the central bank and the government vastly greater abilities to monitor and control our money.

You would use a "wallet" app on your phone to store and spend this money, but that wallet would be tied to your real world identity. The government would be able to see every penny that you spend, when you spent it and who received it. They would also be able to "program" rules into the money. For example, if they wished, they could just drop $1000 into everyone's account with a timer on it. If you didn't spend the $1000 at an approved location within 30 days, then that money would disappear. It's easy to see how this would give them massive control over everything that we do. Using these types of incentives, they could pretty much direct all the flows of money throughout the society.

This would also make it much easier for them to inflate the money supply. No more smoke and mirrors, no more shell games, no more pretending that the central bank is separate from treasury department. They could just create new money and spend it directly.

This kind of control over the money would obviously be a disaster for civil liberties, but it would also be a disaster for the economy. Prices of many things would become pretty meaningless. If the government is dictating spending patterns, then it's not even close to a free market. This means that the prices you see don't represent the real balance between supply and demand. Resources will be misallocated due to the lack of price information in the economy. It may appear to hold steady for a while, but sooner or later it will come crashing down. People will look for other forms of money (a) to protect their purchasing power from inflation; and (b) to be able to buy and sell the things they actually want on the underground free market.

## Gold and Silver in a Digital Age

Gold and silver have been used as money for thousands of years. I personally don't think that's going to change any time soon. There are some extreme crypto advocates who believe that crypto will make gold and silver totally irrelevant as money. Those people believe that gold and silver will come to be regarded purely as industrial metals (like iron or cobalt) and no longer be thought of in any sense as "money".

I don't think that's true. There is no cryptocurrency that can overcome one key advantage of gold and silver, which is that they don't require any infrastructure to "spend". I can hand you a silver coin in exchange for a bag of vegetables without needing any electricity, or Internet access, or a device that can generate a cryptographic signature. To that extent, they will probably always have some roll as a "fallback" currency.

However, that same strength also gives gold and silver a weakness. They are made of hard, heavy, useful stuff. That makes them easy to trust. But it also makes them inconvenient to move around. This is what leads to people storing them in vaults and transacting with paper IOUs.

Some people have suggested that we could use a cryptocurrency to represent real physical ounces of gold and silver. We could move crypto tokens around, secure in the knowledge that there is real metal in a vault somewhere that we can redeem by presenting those crypto tokens. This is a neat idea. It's certainly more efficient to do this with a digital ledger than with physical paper. But the same problem remains. There is no way to know for certain that there is an ounce of physical metal in the vault for every token of the cryptocurrency that supposedly represents the metal. No matter how you slice it, you have to trust someone who promises you that the metal is really there. And since you have to trust someone, there is always an incentive to abuse that trust by only keeping fractional reserves.

Cryptocurrencies that don't claim to be "backed" by physical metal don't have this problem. If you have 10 bitcoins in your wallet, then you have 10 bitcoins. It's provable and visible to everyone. It is rumoured that there are currently around 500 ounces of paper claims on silver for every one ounce of actual physical silver that is available on the COMEX (the main financial exchange for trading commodities). If everyone who thinks they own silver actually tried to get hold of the physical metal, they would quickly discover that there is not enough there to redeem all of the paper claims. In that event, the price of true physical silver would skyrocket as everyone scrambled to get the real stuff so they wouldn't be left holding worthless paper. For the people who already hold physical silver, this would be a huge chance for profit. So why don't a bunch of people get together and demand physical delivery of their silver? That's a long story for another book. Some people have tried to do exactly that in the past. The rumour goes that some government types stepped in and threatened the speculators who tried to take too much silver for physical delivery. Ultimately what makes all of this fraud possible is that silver is big and heavy. It's inconvenient to have 100 pounds of silver dumped on your doorstep. So only relatively few people try to take delivery and it remains possible to issue paper claims that the fraudsters know will never actually need to be fulfilled.

With crypto it's different. Taking your crypto off an exchange and storing it in your own wallet is trivial. It takes a few minutes and you can store any amount you want without needing extra physical space to store it. This makes it much harder to issue false paper claims on crypto. It's much more likely that the owners will demand delivery and the jig will be up.

That is, unless you can make it very expensive and inconvenient to hold crypto directly. This is exactly what has happened with Bitcoin (due to the throughput limit at the high transaction fees). That is why we are seeing more and more people buying Bitcoin but then leaving it on deposit at an exchange instead of taking delivery into their own cryptographic wallet.

## The Next Generation of Crypto

Fundamentally, all of these forms of money have serious problems. CBDCs are a nightmare of inflation, surveillance and financial control. Gold and silver will always be bulky and inconvenient to transport, and therefore vulnerable to the fraud of issuing paper claims for metal that doesn't really exist in the vaults. Bitcoin is looking like it may be vulnerable to the same problem as gold and silver, as expensive transactions incentivise people to store their coins with a custodian. If people don't control their own private keys, they don't control their own crypto. In that case, it becomes possible for whoever *does* control the private keys to set the rules about how they can spend it, to monitor all the owners' transactions and possibly create fake claims on coins that don't really exist.

In my opinion, the best hope we have for an efficient and practical form of money is to look beyond Bitcoin to the next generation of cryptocurrencies. These are projects that are trying to use cryptographic technology to create a form of money that cannot be counterfeited, that cannot be confiscated, that are cheap and easy to hold *directly*, and in some cases are much more difficult for the government to track and monitor.

In the next chapter, we will develop some criteria for identifying cryptocurrency projects that have the potential to be adopted by real people as their preferred form of money.

## Bali: A Case Study in Parallel Currencies

There is one last point that we must consider in order to visualise the future of our monetary systems. Many people in the crypto space are accustomed to speaking as if money is necessarily a zero-sum game. That is, they assume that there can only be one winner. They believe that one cryptocurrency must rise to dominate all the others. This view is called "maximalism". The most common form of this view is "Bitcoin maximalism" which expects Bitcoin to make all other cryptocurrencies basically irrelevant. But there are also maximalists favouring other cryptocurrencies. Maximalists tend to focus in on one area where they see their preferred crypto as being the best. They think that this particular aspect is the most important, and since their preferred crypto is the best in that aspect, it will gradually displace all competitors. But experience tells us that the real world is not like that.

When I visited the Indonesian island of Bali, I learned some first-hand lessons about how money works in the real world. Indonesia has its own currency, the Indonesian rupiah (IDR). In theory, the Indonesian government wants all commerce in Indonesia to be done in their own currency. But in practice, a surprising amount of people in Bali will happily use and accept US dollars. They do this for two reasons. First, tourism is a big industry in Bali. Many tourists arrive with US dollars in their possession since those are easier to obtain in their home country than Indonesian rupiah. If you want to attract customers then it makes sense to accept the currency that is most convenient for them. Second, the US dollar, for all its flaws, is still a more stable currency than the Indonesian rupiah. People in Bali can preserve more of their purchasing power by holding US dollars than by holding rupiah. They still need to hold *some* rupiah, but it makes sense for Balinese people to use both rupiah *and* dollars in different contexts.

What was most surprising is that it was not just the common people in Bali who would sometimes accept US dollars. Even the government agents at the airport were willing to accept US dollars from arriving travellers (who were required to pay a fee to the government upon arrival). Even though it is clearly in the Indonesian government's interest to have all commerce conducted in Rupiah, they themselves had still chosen to accept US dollars in some circumstances.

What is the lesson here? The lesson is that two currencies *can* exist side by side in the same area and the same economy. Cryptocurrency does not have to completely replace fiat currency in order to become established as a common form of money. If cryptocurrencies solve real, practical problems for people, then they can have a significant role in the economy even if fiat, gold and silver don't completely go away.

It also means that multiple cryptocurrencies may become established as the preferred form of money in different sectors of the economy. Cryptos that focus on privacy above all else will likely be the preferred money in contexts where market participants are very privacy sensitive, such as dark net markets (DNMs). If you are dealing in goods and services that are fully or partially illegal[7] then you will definitely be willing to put up with higher transaction fees or a less convenient wallet experience if it means that you lower your risk of being arrested. On the other hand, if you are operating in a sector where customers are very sensitive to delays then you will likely prefer a currency that sacrifices some privacy features in favour of guaranteeing speed. One example would be high-frequency traders moving funds between exchanges for arbitrage. A less technical example would be a business operating a lot of vending machines or drive-through food services. These are contexts where customers are in a hurry and are very sensitive to delays in completing the transaction.

On the one hand, maximalists have a point. It is inefficient for an economy to have a thousand different types of money in circulation (in that case, you're basically back to a barter system). So yes, we will probably move to a relatively small number of circulating forms of money over time. But there is no guarantee that we will reach the point where

---

7   Remember that "illegal" does not necessarily mean "immoral". The same black market that provides drugs and prostitution in the United States also provides food in Venezuela and Bibles in Dubai.

everyone is using a single currency for every transaction. Real world experience tells us that multiple currencies often circulate side by side when they are more convenient for specific uses.

# Investing Wisely

If we are going to be wise investors and speculators then we need to understand what role cryptocurrency plays in our personal portfolio. There is no single "correct" way to structure a portfolio. It depends on the goals of the investor. This book is called *Crypto for Conservatives*, but that does not mean that you have to be building a "conservative" portfolio with ultra-low risk. What it means is that you approach investing with wisdom and with your eyes wide open. You know what you are buying, you know why you are buying it, and any risks that you take are deliberate and calculated. This is the opposite of being a naive speculator whose strategy is hardly distinguishable from gambling.

If you are young and have a long time frame ahead of you, you may be trying to structure a relatively aggressive portfolio, seeking high growth and accepting some higher risks. If you are older and mainly looking to preserve the wealth that you have already built up then you will likely want a portfolio with lower risk, while also accepting less potential growth. As such, nothing in this book should be taken as financial advice. All of this information is for general educational purposes. It is designed to help you think clearly about the cryptocurrency space and make informed decisions. But they will always be *your* decisions and *your* responsibility.

## How Risky is Cryptocurrency?

How risky is it to include cryptocurrency in your portfolio? History tells us that it can be quite risky. Sometimes you will hear hardcore Bitcoin bulls say things like "Bitcoin has been the single best performing asset in the world over the last 10 years." That makes it sound like Bitcoin has a consistent track record of performance, as though it always goes up in value. But that leaves out some extremely important details. Yes, since it was created, Bitcoin's price has been on a long-term upward trend. But the pull backs have been brutal at many points.

There was a bull market that ended around December 2017. During this run, the price of Bitcoin went from just over $1,000 in January 2017 to almost $19,500 in December 2017. That's almost a 20X increase inside a single year. That's a 2000% return. People who bought at $1,000 looked like geniuses. But the majority of that increase came within just one month from November to December. In that time, the price went from $6,000 to $19,000. People who were watching Bitcoin buyers get rich jumped on the bandwagon. They bought in at $12,000 in early

December and made a 50% return on their money in just *two weeks*. Even though they had bought Bitcoin at the all-time highest price, they were still making money hand over fist.

Then the pull back came. In the next month and a half, the Bitcoin price got down to around $7,000. People who bought at $12,000 in early December were up 50% by mid December. But then by February, those who hadn't sold at the top were actually *down* 40% on their original investment. I'm sure some people told them not to worry, to just hold on and that things would turn around. This is the investment of a lifetime, they would say, this price drop is just a setback. But the drop continued. By December 2018 (one year later), the Bitcoin price was down around $3,700. People who bought in during the late stage of the bull run at $12,000 were now down 70% on their original investment. Even worse, there were some suckers who bought it at the absolute peak around $19,000. They were down as much as 80%.

If you had put your hard-earned money into an investment and then seen the value of that investment go down by 80% in a single year, would you still hold on to it? The vast majority of people would not. They would sell, get off the rollercoaster and lick their wounds.

However, if you had stuck with it, you would ultimately have been okay. If you bought Bitcoin at the $19,000 peak and held onto it, you would be up 300% on your original money by mid-2021, only 3.5 years later. Managing 300% returns in 3.5 years is still a great achievement. But imagine you had sold when you were 70-80% down, thinking that it was the end and that the whole thing was going to keep crashing to zero. Then you watched over the next few years as Bitcoin hit new all time highs. You could have tripled your money, but instead you lost 80% of it.

I am painting this picture for you to drive home the point that cryptocurrency speculation is not for the faint of heart. In the long term, it *is* possible that the purchasing power of a cryptocurrency can go to zero. If a fiat currency can be abandoned because people adopt something else that is more convenient, then the same thing can theoretically happen to a cryptocurrency. Because cryptocurrencies are not used to manufacture products (like gold and silver are), if a cryptocurrency is not used *as* a currency, then it won't be used at all.

But even setting aside that extreme scenario, it's simply a volatile market. There may well be times when the value of your cryptocurrency assets drops 50% in the space of a month. If you go "all in" on cryptocurrency, the emotional weight of that volatility could be intense. For most people, it will be much more comfortable to have cryptocurrency be only a small part of your larger investment portfolio. If you are quite risk averse, then cryptocurrency should only be a tiny part. If you are prepared to take some risks for the chance of higher returns, then it can be larger. Part of being a wise investor is being honest with yourself about what risks you are emotionally prepared to handle (and anyone who depends on you, like your spouse or your kids).

## The Unique Opportunity of Cryptocurrency

Now that we have talked about the risk, let's talk seriously about the upside. What are the reasons that you would want to have cryptocurrency in your portfolio?

To understand that, you need to think in terms of asset classes. An investment portfolio can usually be divided up into a few broad categories. Here is a basic framework that you can use for classifying assets.

## Growth Assets

These are things you hold because you think that they are going to increase in market dominance. A key example is tech companies like Netflix or Zoom. If you predicted the trend that more and more people would start working from home during the Covid-19 lockdowns, then buying shares in Zoom would have been a great move. As more people do their meetings over the Internet, Zoom's market gets bigger and they earn way more revenue. A tech company may not have that much revenue today, but their market can expand very quickly if their product goes viral, so they may scale up very quickly over a short time frame. These types of investments tend to have higher risk but also give higher rewards.

## Value Assets

These are things that you hold because of the value they already have, rather than because of some future value they might potentially gain. This would be things like stocks that are paying solid dividends or real estate that is producing a rental income. For low-risk investors, this is the bread and butter. Assets that produce a steady income give you stability.

## Cash and Liquid Assets

The final category is cash and other types of liquid assets. This would include things like bonds that have a relatively stable market price. These are things that you hold for the purpose of flexibility. If there is a sudden market crash, having these assets in your portfolio (a) partially protects you from the crash; and (b) puts you in a good position to quickly buy up some of the struggling growth and value assets while they are cheap.

## Where Does Cryptocurrency Fit In?

This is what is so exciting about cryptocurrency as an investment class. On the one hand, cryptocurrency is a growth asset. As more people use it for commerce, the network effect grows and the value of the currency increases. There are many features and technological innovations to improve people's lives that can be built around cryptocurrencies. These gradually create more incentive for people to adopt the cryptocurrency in daily life, which pushes up the market demand to hold the currency.

So far so good. Crypto looks like a growth asset, not a value asset.

But crypto can also potentially function as a form of "cash" or liquid asset. To be fair, it does not perform that way today. When other growth assets crash, cryptocurrencies tend to crash right alongside them. To that extent, cryptocurrency has not historically done very well at preserving your purchasing power when growth assets crash.

However, as adoption of cryptocurrencies continues, this should become less and less the case. If we reach a point where most people you know are using cryptocurrency to buy something every week, then crypto will be starting to look a lot less like a speculative investment and a lot more like plain and simple *money*. At that point, we can fully expect it to protect us against crashes in growth assets. People still need to eat. And if the main way they do that is by spending crypto on food, then crypto is not going to lose a lot of purchasing power just because some stocks are down.

Crypto is an undeveloped growth asset today that has the potential to become a liquid cash asset in the future. That means there is potential to reap the benefit of two asset classes in one – *if* we can pick the cryptos that end up with the widest practical adoption in real world commerce.

# How 100X Growth Is Possible

For most people, cash is fiat currency. This is what people use to buy and sell things in their daily lives. People will always want to hold some cash because it protects them from uncertainty. If you hold cash, you can quickly exchange it for anything else you need *once you know that you need it*. If you keep all of your wealth in other assets, then exchanging is a slower process, which makes your life more frustrating. That's why there is always demand to hold cash, because it is a convenient medium of exchange.

The worldwide market cap of cash is estimated at around $100 trillion USD. To put that number in perspective, the market cap of gold is only about $10 trillion USD. The cash market is huge.

If we were going to move into a world where just 1% of global cash transactions were done in a particular cryptocurrency rather than fiat, we would be looking at a potential market cap of $1 trillion USD for that crypto. The market cap of Bitcoin (BTC) is actually already at $1 trillion USD on its own. But Bitcoin is handling way less than 1% of the world's transactions, even accounting for the Lightning Network. What this tells me is that speculation can push the market cap of a cryptocurrency way out ahead of its actual adoption in people's lives. This is one of the reasons that I actually don't hold Bitcoin in my own portfolio, but more on that later.

One of the cryptocurrencies that I do hold in my own portfolio is Bitcoin Cash. The market cap of Bitcoin Cash is somewhere around $10 *billion* USD. Not trillion, *billion*. Suppose we were going to move into a world where just 1% of all transactions were done in Bitcoin Cash, a world where 1% of all cash balances were held in this particular cryptocurrency. We would then expect the market cap of this one crypto to be somewhere around 1% of the global cash market, which would be $1 trillion USD. That's a 100X increase from the market cap that Bitcoin Cash has today. Now, I'm not claiming that this scenario is definitely going to happen. But it's not totally absurd either, especially if you're looking 5 or 10 years down the road. Even if Bitcoin Cash were to become just 0.1% of global transactions, that would still suggest a 10X increase in price from where it is today. Is it really that hard to see 0.1% of the world's transactions being done in system that has proven itself to be fast, secure and reliable, with ultra low fees and no delays for crossing international borders? I don't think it's that crazy to imagine it happening.

That's why there's such big potential for growth in the crypto market. If you can find cryptos that have proven they can create a lot of convenience in people's lives *and* have a disproportionately low market cap compared to their prospects for future adoption, then you are looking at a legitimate opportunity.

## Criteria for Evaluating a Cryptocurrency

So how do we decide which cryptocurrencies should be in our portfolio? First of all, we need to find a balance between diversification and selectiveness. We could just allocate 1% each to the top 100 cryptocurrencies on the market. That would give us broad diversification. If there is a cryptocurrency that is going to eventually dominate the market, then chances are good (though not definite) that it is already in the top 100 by market cap. However, the harsh reality is that a lot of those cryptocurrencies are likely to fail and collapse in value. On the one hand, we want some diversity, because it's extraordinarily difficult to know exactly which form of money the market will ultimately prefer. But on the other hand, we don't want to buy every crypto under the sun because we will be putting good money into a lot of projects that almost certainly aren't going to succeed.

This situation is not unique.

During the dot-com boom of the 1990s, investors would buy stock in just about any company that had a flashy sales pitch and a nice domain name. Many of those companies had terrible business models and went nowhere. They were just cashing in on the FOMO ("fear of missing out") that investors were feeling about this new Internet-based sector of the economy. The cryptocurrency world is the same. There is a lot of stuff out there that is, frankly, trash. It's not going to go anywhere. But since Bitcoin has produced such huge returns over the last decade, people can pitch their coin, tell you that it's going to give 100X returns and not sound totally insane. After all, if Bitcoin did it, then how do we know that this other coin won't do the same, especially if we get in early?

People who succeeded during the dot-com boom were the ones who could see through the glitter, who avoided the trash and who bought solid companies with real business models. Companies like Amazon were around back then. They were part of the boom. And when the boom ended, their stock price took a brief hit along with everything else. But they survived the crash, kept going and still turned out to be one of the most profitable investments that their buyers ever made.

To invest in cryptocurrency wisely, we need to evaluate the various opportunities through a set of filters. Those filters are designed to eliminate the trash and make sure that our portfolios only contain cryptocurrencies that actually have a legitimate chance of gaining widespread adoption for a practical purpose.

# Filtering out the Trash

In this next chapter, I'll be introducing you to the filters that I personally use to keep the trash out of my own portfolio. Before I will buy any non-trivial amount of a cryptocurrency, it needs to get a passing grade on every single one of these tests. It doesn't necessarily need to be the absolute best in every category. There is no cryptocurrency that is best-in-class on every metric, since they each make different trade-offs. But to be in my portfolio, a cryptocurrency must not utterly fail on any one of these points because I consider them to be show-stoppers for mass adoption.

## How Difficult is it to *Actually Use?*

The first test is powerful because of its simplicity. How difficult is this cryptocurrency to actually use? If it's difficult to use, then people won't use it. Software that is overly frustrating, or requires an engineering degree to operate, will never get mass adoption. If it doesn't get adopted, then it won't have any long-term value. It's as simple as that.

Go on the app store of your choice, as long as it's the Apple's app store or the Google Play store. Other app stores don't count because they will never get you mass adoption[8]. If there are no apps for using this crypto in the two major app stores, it's already failed the test.

What if you have the reverse situation? What if there are 100 apps for this cryptocurrency in the app store? How do you know which one to choose? I would recommend searching for a few articles online and making a list of the top five wallet apps for this crypto that seem to be mentioned or recommended the most often. Don't be afraid to try all five. You might only like one or two, but you don't want to write off a crypto just because you personally didn't like the interface on one particular app. Not everyone has the same tastes as you do. But if all five are terrible, then that's a strong sign that the terrible parts are "baked in" as part of the underlying crypto technology and they will always be terrible. If at least a couple of the apps give you a smooth user experience then a smooth user experience is at least *possible*, and we can move on to the next filter.

---

8    I don't relish saying this! I don't like living in a world where Apple and Google can effectively be gatekeepers over what software people run. But at the same time, I am realistic about it. Normal people don't jailbreak phones or install alternative app stores.

How do you test a crypto app? Simple. Get a little bit of the currency and try sending it back and forth between two wallets. If that's difficult to do, then this crypto fails the test. If you're lucky, the crypto you are testing will have a "faucet" website somewhere so that you can get a small amount for free. Crypto communities create faucets specifically to help people take their favourite crypto for a spin. If you can get some free coins from a faucet, that's usually a very good sign. It means that the existing users of that crypto are willing to put their money where their mouth is so that you can test out what they have to offer. One crypto that has a lot of faucets available is Nano (XNO). This is partly because Nano has zero transaction fees, which makes it very easy to distribute small amounts for testing.

If you can't find a faucet, then you can buy a few dollars worth on your favourite exchange. If the coin is not available on any major exchange, then my advice is to just walk away and consider the test failed. If it ever does get listed on a major exchange, then you can come back and try this test again. Your decision doesn't have to be set in stone. But if it's not even on a major exchange yet, then it's nowhere near ready to be considered for my personal portfolio.

One final point is to make sure that any wallet apps you are testing are "non-custodial". That is to say that the wallet app lets you hold your own private keys (they are not in someone else's custody). Always remember: *not your keys, not your coins*. Some wallet apps seem really slick and easy to use, but this is because you are giving up control of your money to the people who made the wallet. They can make everything appear very smooth because they are handling the tricky parts in the background. But that also means you are letting the creators of the wallet app be the "custodians" of your money. This power means that they may freeze your account or steal your funds at any moment. This defeats the whole purpose of cryptocurrency. So if there are no good wallet apps that let you *hold your own private keys*, then it's a failing grade on this test.

## Can I Spend It Somewhere?

This is the next most obvious test. If a cryptocurrency is going to get mainstream adoption in daily commerce, then it has to be easy for merchants to start accepting it as payment. What's the best way to see if it's easy for merchants to accept it? Check and see if any merchants are accepting it already. If there are a lot of merchants accepting it, that tells you that it must not be all that difficult to get started. It also tells you that there are probably some customers requesting to be able to pay with that particular cryptocurrency. Finally, it's a good indicator that the community around that cryptocurrency has people in it who are willing to volunteer their time to help merchants get set up and start accepting it.

If you search around the web (especially around the Reddit community for a particular coin) but it's still very difficult to find any merchants accepting a cryptocurrency, that's a red flag. If you find none, then I would suggest staying away until the ecosystem around that crypto is at least mature enough to have a few merchants involved.

Another test that you can do (but which takes a bit more effort) is to try selling something for that cryptocurrency yourself. If you have a brick-and-mortar business then you can try getting set up to accept payments from your customers (you don't necessarily need a real customer who wants to pay with that crypto yet – you can be your own customer for testing purposes). If getting set up to accept that cryptocurrency is a very difficult for you to do, then it will be difficult for others as well. If it's easy, then it will be easy for others. You can also do this if you have an online business. Set up your website to accept payments in the crypto you are testing. If you set up your website to accept payments then you should post about it in a Reddit group for that cryptocurrency. You are very likely to get a few enthusiasts who are willing to buy something from you just to try it out and to encourage you for your efforts. This will help you see how difficult it is to start accepting a particular crypto in real world commerce. In my experience, the gold standard in this arena is Bitcoin Cash (BCH). You can download an app called "Bitcoin Cash Register" on any iOS or Android device. You create a wallet address, put it in that app, and you're away. You can start accepting BCH payments over the counter at your business. In my experience, very few cryptocurrencies can boast an "onboarding" experience that is so simple. And it shows. A quick tour of Reddit or YouTube will quickly show you loads of videos of merchants who accept payments through the Bitcoin Cash Register app.

## Is the Issuance Policy Acceptable?

The next test that we use to filter out trashy projects is to understand their issuance policy. How are the coins created and distributed? How quickly does this process occur? How "fair" is the distribution mechanism?

Remember, one of the main advantages of cryptocurrency is that it gets us out of the realm of fiat money. The reason we wanted to get out of fiat money in the first place is because of the terrible issuance policies forced upon us by governments. The government can issue more fiat money into their own pockets any time they want. That's how they rig the game and that's exactly the sort of problem we are trying to fix. So if a cryptocurrency has an issuance policy that gives certain people an unfair advantage, that's definitely something that we want to avoid.

Issuance policies in the crypto space vary a lot, so figuring out the issuance policy of a particular coin requires us to do some research. This can usually be done by looking up a primary website for the project and reading up on the background details.

In my own portfolio, I refuse to own any cryptocurrencies that continuously emit new coins into the pockets of people who are not actively and continually contributing to the network. The Bitcoin network, for example, only emits coins to people who are directly contributing to the live network by running mining software. The Firo network (formerly called Zcoin) is different. Of all the coins emitted on the Firo network, 15% go to a "development fund" controlled by its creators. In theory, the purpose of this fund is to pay for ongoing development of the software used by the network nodes. That might seem reasonable on the surface, but I have two major objections. First, there is no guarantee that further development work will actually happen. If the community is dissatisfied with the work being done then there is no way for them to stop paying that 15% to the founders. The creators can theoretically just sit back and collect their 15% for free, forever. Second, I think that 15% of all the money ever created is way too high of a price tag to pay for ongoing development of the software. If Firo actually gets wide mainstream adoption as a primary global currency, that 15% would make the founders disproportionately wealthy on an obscene scale. None of the richest people or corporations on Earth today come anywhere close to receiving 15% of the money in circulation on an ongoing basis. The only organisations that pull those kind of numbers are governments, which routinely suck that much out of the society through taxes. That's exactly the sort of thing I'm trying to get away from. That's why I got into crypto in the first place! So, in spite of some very interesting and innovative privacy technology, I'm steering clear of Firo for my investing portfolio.

## What are the *Internal* Political Risks?

Every crypto project has some kind of governance structure. It may be quite formal and well-defined or it may be very informal and fluid. On the formal end of the spectrum, there may be a legal entity (like a foundation or a corporation) that manages the project. At the more informal end, the project might be run by volunteers who have influence over the project arising organically from the merit of their contributions. Whatever form it takes, there is always *some* kind of governance. Decisions are made and only humans can make them.

To understand whether a given cryptocurrency is a good investment, we need to understand the governance structure. If the power to determine the future direction of the project is concentrated in only a few people's hands, then there is a risk that they could leverage that power to their own benefit in a way that undermines the value of our investment. On the other hand, if the power to determine the future direction is extremely spread out, then the project may struggle with a lack of a unifying vision. If there are conflicting agendas among the community then there can be vigorous (and even spiteful) debates among contributors. That kind of community friction can create uncertainty for investors about which direction things will ultimately go. Some examples will make this clearer.

On the very formal end of the spectrum, you have coins like Firo, which has a corporation responsible for overseeing development. The corporation receives part of all the coins that are mined in order to fund their operations.

Slightly less formal is Nano. Instead of a corporation, development is overseen by a non-profit entity called the Nano Foundation. The Nano Foundation does not receive any cut of newly minted coins (there is no ongoing creation of new coins in Nano anyway!), but they do accept voluntary donations from the community to support their work. Development of the main Nano node software is largely coordinated by the Nano Foundation.

Another step less formal would be Bitcoin (BTC). While there is technically no corporation or foundation that explicitly oversees development of the Bitcoin node software, there are very established people and organisations who are the *de facto* custodians. There is really only one node implementation that is used in practice, which is called "Bitcoin Core". There are a team of people who have the authority to accept or reject submissions for changes to the official Bitcoin Core node software. If the people in that inner circle reject the changes proposed by a developer, then those changes will likely never be used widely in the community. This makes the Bitcoin Core team functional gatekeepers around the implementation of the Bitcoin node software. In practice, the members of the Bitcoin Core team tend to be employed by a small number of institutions. One key example is a VC-backed corporation called Blockstream. Because several Bitcoin Core maintainers work for Blockstream, concerns have been raised in the past that the commercial interests of that company may have an outsized influence on the development of the Bitcoin Core node software.

Taking yet another step away from formal structure is the Monero project. Monero, like Bitcoin or Nano, has a single dominant implementation that is used by virtually everyone who interacts with the network. Development of the Monero software (both the node and the official wallets) are overseen by a core team of maintainers. However, in contrast to Bitcoin, development on the Monero project tends to be more often funded by contributions from the community of users rather than from corporate interests. The Monero project includes the Monero CCS (Community Crowdfunding System). Anyone can create a CCS proposal where they propose to do a set of defined work on the project and ask the community to donate money to pay them for their efforts. For example, a recent proposal was created by a developer to add a feature called "view tag scanning" which dramatically improves the speed at which a Monero wallet is able to scan the network for incoming transactions. This proposal was quickly funded by donations from the community through the CCS. The developer submitted the changes to the core maintainers who then go on to review it for issues before formally accepting those changes into the next official release. The core maintainers themselves also commonly put up CCS proposals to fund their personal salaries. This emphasis on community involvement in the funding process is hoped keep the priorities of development focused on the needs of the grassroots users.

Finally, with extremely informal governance, is the Bitcoin Cash project. After the original Bitcoin chain split into Bitcoin (BTC) and Bitcoin Cash (BCH) versions, there was significant animosity in the Bitcoin Cash community toward what many perceived as the excessive influence of Blockstream over the direction of the Bitcoin project. Many felt that the artificial throughput limit was pushed so hard because it was beneficial to Blockstream's business model, rather than being beneficial to the end users and their need to have fast, cheap, reliable transactions. For these historical reasons, the Bitcoin Cash community tends to be very sceptical of any one organisation having too much say over the direction of the project. Where every other project mentioned above has a single dominant node implementation, Bitcoin Cash has at least six different, independent implementations that are in active use and development (Bitcoin Cash Node, Bitcoin Unlimited, BCHD, Bitcoin Verde, Flowee and Knuth). Each of these projects has their own independent governance structure and all of them are run on the same network by different participants for their own reasons. Most miners tend to run Bitcoin Cash Node. But many of the end users, service providers and payment gateways prefer to use one of the the other implementations which offer more convenient features for their own use cases. The result is an *extremely* robust, diverse and decentralised ecosystem. Software developers who want to try making new improvements to the node software do not need to get approval from any core team of maintainers to release their changes to a substantial audience. For example, the BCHD team was able to implement "fast sync" technology in their node (which dramatically reduces the time to bring a fresh new node online). They did not need developers from any other implementation to agree with this idea before they could try it on a few production systems and release it for any other interested users to try (including this author). The flip side is that this openness to letting anyone contribute changes and try them out can lead to tension. A change like BCHD's fast-sync is not really controversial because it has no noticeable effect on users of other node implementations. But there have been serious schisms in the community when stakeholders have pushed more radical agendas. When Craig Wright and nChain were pushing for a permanent freeze on all protocol changes, the result was that they were overruled by the larger BCH community and decided to fork away onto their own chain called Bitcoin SV (Satoshi's Vision). When Amaury Séchet and BitcoinABC tried to push for a fraction of all future mining rewards to be paid to a few privileged developers rather than to the miners, the community reacted strongly and this event led to the creation of Bitcoin Cash Node as a replacement for the BitcoinABC software. The BitcoinABC team then forked away and created their own new currency called "eCash". When there is this level of decentralisation, the progress of the project can certainly appear chaotic. Nevertheless, the shared ethos of pursuing "digital cash for the world" has so far kept the Bitcoin Cash community fairly strong and cohesive. Still, a lot of human capital is consumed in these heated debates. That effort might theoretically be spent on more productive tasks (like research, development and marketing) if the governance structure had been more formal and rigid.

As you can see, each of these structures poses their own unique risks. I myself tend to be more comfortable with projects that have relatively informal structures built mainly around meritocracy. It reassures me to know that there are passionate, mission-driven contributors who stand ready to take matters into their own hands and "rescue" the project if bad actors try to take it over for their own ends. But others may disagree with my assessment. Others may think that the "benevolent dictator" model of a project with more formal control is a more appropriate way to protect their investment. The choice is up to you. But it's worth knowing something about the history and ethos of the project's key contributors before adding a cryptocurrency token to your portfolio. As an example, I have never added Bitcoin SV or eCash to my portfolio because I have strong objections to the way that the major players behind those projects behaved during their respective splits from Bitcoin Cash. I think there is too much risk that the leaders of those projects will make decisions that benefit their own back pocket in the short term rather than benefiting the broader community in the long term.

# What Are the *External* Political Risks?

Having covered internal politics, it's now time to consider external politics. In particular, is this project at risk of being attacked or suppressed by various governments? Sometimes you hear people throw out a sweeping statement like "governments will ban crypto". The truth is much more nuanced than that. This issue is very complex and could fill an entire book of its own. For our purposes, we will just look at a few examples to help you understand the concept of external risks.

Bitcoin (BTC) is the cryptocurrency with the largest market cap, now well over $1 trillion USD. It has become a non-trivial part of the economy in many countries. There are Bitcoin ETFs traded on major stock exchanges, there are multi-billion dollar corporations with Bitcoin on their balance sheets, there are many companies employing an army of people whose businesses revolve around Bitcoin. If major Western governments all banned Bitcoin ownership tomorrow, they would probably find themselves in a world of hurt. A huge number of voters would be up in arms because a chunk of their investment portfolio had been taken away at the stroke of a pen. Masses of people in the industry would be out of work. It would be a huge political thunderstorm. For that reason, banning it outright is extremely unlikely to happen.

But what about regulating it towards a slow death? That's much more likely.

Bitcoin mining currently uses a monumental amount of electricity. Even though there is a very nuanced discussion to be had about how that energy is sourced[9], it's easy to see how the political class can spin the simple fact of Bitcoin's energy usage into a call for it to be regulated. If they play the climate-change card hard enough, they will probably be able to introduce a whole slew of mining regulations. Because Bitcoin is mined using very specialised computers (called ASICs), it is almost exclusively mined in large data centres, rather than by individuals in their own homes. This makes it very easy for government agents to find where the mining

---

9   Cryptocurrency miners are actually pretty agnostic about the source of their electricity. They are just as happy to use solar, wind, hydro, nuclear or geothermal power as they are to use fossil fuels. Some have even argued that cryptocurrency mining may enable non-fossil-fuel energy to become *more* economically viable since mining can use excess energy that would otherwise be wasted. This allows energy producers to stabilise the balance between their fluctuating supply and the available demand.

is being done and send men with guns to the data centre. The government may try to compel these large mining companies to refuse to process transactions involving blacklisted addresses (i.e. addresses known to belong to people the government doesn't like). If you are buying Bitcoin for the "censorship resistance" feature, then the risk of government-regulated mining should be a serious concern for you.

On the other hand, there are cryptocurrencies like Monero that don't have this particular problem. Monero is mined using general-purpose CPUs, not specialised ASIC hardware. This makes it much easier for individuals to mine Monero using their own PC at home. It also makes it much more difficult to figure out who is doing the mining. The result is that it is dramatically more difficult for the government to regulate Monero mining. Additionally, Monero's ledger is much more private, such that miners cannot identify who is sending and receiving the transactions. Even if there were an attempt to regulate Monero mining, it may not actually be possible to effectively blacklist transactions.

In many ways, these features of Monero are great for censorship resistance. However, they put Monero in the crosshairs for a different type of risk. In several countries now, including Australia and the UK, it is no longer possible to buy Monero directly on a regulated exchange. While it is not illegal for individuals to own Monero in those countries, the regulated exchanges have been pressured by their banking partners not to make Monero available for trading. If the exchanges want to keep doing business in those countries then they need to have access to the fiat banking system. But they can only keep that access if they play ball. Because Monero is quite private, it has been easier for governments to paint Monero as a "coin for criminals". On this basis, they have been able to make it quite difficult for average users to obtain Monero because it is no longer available through the usual channels (regulated exchanges). It is still easy for advanced users to obtain Monero, it just requires a few extra steps. But this removal from traditional exchanges does present a challenge for adoption by the masses.

Hopefully this contrast between Bitcoin and Monero shows you the principle here. Different coins have different properties which make them vulnerable in subtly different ways to interference by hostile governments. Before adding a cryptocurrency to your portfolio, it's worth understanding what those vulnerabilities are and forming your own assessment of the risks.

# What are the Technical Risks?

Having covered the political risks, we need to go a step deeper into the project internals and understand the technical risks. This part can be intimidating (or even seem impossible) for many investors. How can we understand what might go wrong with the engineering of a cryptocurrency network if we don't personally have an engineering background?

If you are in that boat, don't worry too much about it. The Internet is filled with serious enthusiasts who are much more hardcore about cryptocurrency than you. Many of them are ready to give their opinion about technical issues. If you look on the right online forums, you can find endless technical discussions about the fine details of how particular cryptocurrencies are implemented. You don't actually have to go as far as reading through all of the code yourself. Of course, wading through all of that online discussion might also require more technical background than you possess. This will be true for most people. But again, if you ask nicely in the right forum, there will usually be someone ready and willing to give you a summary of key points. You can also consider whether some of these risks have actually caused problems in the past and then ask whether the causes of those problems have since been addressed by the developers, or whether the same problem is just waiting to happen again.

Since this filter could once again fill a book of its own, we will look at one key example just to establish what kinds of things you are looking for in order to evaluate technical risks.

One key area of technical risk that is shared by virtually all cryptocurrencies is how they will cope with *scaling*. A cryptocurrency might seem to work very smoothly when there are only a handful of transactions being processed every minute. But what happens when it starts trying to handle a bigger load? What happens when usage climbs up to 10 TPS (transactions per second)? What about 100 TPS? A cryptocurrency that is going to handle mainstream adoption will *eventually* need to be able to handle at least 1,000 TPS (which is roughly 1% of global cash transaction volume, or about half of what PayPal currently handles). But no cryptocurrency has anywhere close to that level of adoption just yet. It should also be remembered that computing resources (like disk space and bandwidth) will likely become much cheaper as time goes on, which makes the cost of scaling the network much more affordable. Nevertheless, if you are evaluating a cryptocurrency and you find that is already struggling to handle 10 TPS or 100 TPS, then you have reason to be concerned.

Bitcoin BTC deliberately does not handle even 10 TPS on its main network, let alone 100 or 1000. To achieve that kind of scale you have to transition to the Lightning Network (and deal with the complications that you find there).

Bitcoin Cash has shown in practice that its technology can already handle processing 1,000 TPS on a small computer like a Raspberry Pi 4. This has been demonstrated using their "scale net", which is a testing environment for developing the software. The scale net processes transactions just like the main network, but the coins are essentially given out for free by the maintainers so that people can use them for testing the network. Clearly scaling is a great strength area for Bitcoin Cash, which makes sense given that it has been one of their key areas of focus.

Nano may potentially be even *more* capable of handling high throughput than Bitcoin Cash. Nano is named precisely because it is designed to be the most small and efficient protocol for simple, direct transfers from one person to another. On the one hand, Nano's throughput is theoretically unlimited. Transactions are processed individually instead of being grouped into periodic blocks. So the only real throughput limit is the processing power of the "representative nodes" which vote on transactions. Nano has come under spam attacks in the past and this has, as a side effect, demonstrated that the Nano main network (not a test network) can process well in excess of 100 TPS without any issues. However, there is a drawback to this architecture. Because Nano is based on voting, it can only go as fast as the *slowest* representative node that is required to reach a consensus vote. If the deciding vote is being done by a node that is suffering performance problems or has gone offline then the whole network can be slowed down while faster nodes wait for votes from slower nodes. This is in contrast to a traditional proof-of-work blockchain architecture which is purposely designed to be asynchronous and not dependent on the actions of any particular node. There is also the possibility that the majority of the network will keep up, while particular individual nodes will fall behind. In the most recent serious spam attack, this problem manifested and some slower nodes fell behind the rest of the network. This resulted in some users reporting that they had to wait hours or days for their (normally instant) transactions to be processed. Improving the handling of such spam attacks is currently a primary goal of ongoing Nano development. Nano's architecture is very promising, but there are still some issues that need to be resolved in order for a throughput rate of 1,000 TPS to be viable on the main network.

On the other end of the spectrum is Monero. The trade-off for all of Monero's excellent privacy features is that Monero has a bigger scaling problem than other cryptocurrencies. Precisely because of the privacy features, transactions in Monero require more bytes of disk space to store. This really adds up over time. Additionally, since Monero is so private, there is no way to know which coins have already been spent and which have not. This means that old transaction data cannot be "pruned" and discarded in the way that it can for cryptocurrencies like Bitcoin Cash and Nano. While there is some limited pruning possible, it is fundamentally necessary in Monero to retain access to every transaction ever created in order to be able to validate all possible future transactions. This may present some real difficulties at scale. Not just in the disk space required to store the ledger, but also in the processing power required to validate new transactions, which may easily reference historic data from several years prior. Nevertheless, the Monero community is very aware of the challenges around scaling and devotes considerable effort to innovating in this area. Monero has pioneered scaling technologies like their "adaptive block weight" algorithm, which helps incentivise miners to find an optimal balance between increasing throughput to help the end users while also keeping the throughput rate from increasing too quickly and bloating the ledger for node operators.

Hopefully this sketch has given you a sense different cryptocurrency designs come with their own engineering trade-offs. While it may seem intimidating to try and evaluate these issues if you are not a computer science major, it doesn't have to be a big deal. If you are at least a "power user" who knows your way around a computer, then the best way to apply this filter is to try setting up a node for yourself. How much effort is required to get the node software working? How much disk space and bandwidth is required to run the node? How many TPS is that cryptocurrency currently handling? If it is only handling a few TPS today, but it's already difficult for a modern computer to handle the load, then that's a clear indication that scaling is going to be a difficult issue going forward.

# How Private Are My Transactions?

Having mentioned Monero's trade-off between privacy and scalability, this is a good time to talk more about the privacy dimension. Privacy in cryptocurrency matters for two basic reasons. The first is that people don't like being stalked. If you've ever had someone snoop on you by looking up your Facebook profile then you know the feeling. How would you like it if a person you just met could look you up online and see bits and pieces of your bank statement? People don't want their financial dealings to be made public for the same reason that they keep curtains on their bedroom windows. Some things just aren't other people's business.

The other reason that privacy matters is *fungibility*, a term that we mentioned in an earlier chapter. For money to be as useful as possible, people need to be able to accept it at face value. Every unit needs to have the same exchange value as every other unit. If your crypto can be traced to some illegal or frowned-upon activity then it will be harder to spend. People might not want to touch it. Privacy helps create fungibility. If the money is private, then it can't really be associated with some "bad" activity. That property of fungibility makes the money easier to use in day to day transactions because we don't have to worry about accidentally accepting "tainted" coins.

Privacy in cryptocurrency exists on a wide spectrum. There are a variety of different ways that crypto engineers try to achieve privacy and they each come with different tradeoffs. There are basically three things that we are trying to hide: the amount of the transaction, the recipient and the sender. Some cryptocurrencies hide all three, while others only hide one or two of these elements.

Zcash and related cryptocurrencies (like Pirate Chain) make a good effort at hiding all three with strong encryption. But the techniques used for achieving this privacy require a "trusted setup" process. Essentially, there were about 70 people involved in generating some numbers with different computers, which they then allegedly destroyed. These numbers are the encryption base. If you trust those 70 people, everything is fine. But if those 70 people happened to not be trustworthy, then it is possible that someone, somewhere actually has a backdoor into that cryptocurrency. Personally, I am not prepared to take that chance. Trusted setup is a deal breaker for me. So in spite of the theoretically strong encryption, I prefer to look elsewhere.

Monero hides all three elements through a combination of technologies: "range proofs" to hide the amount, "stealth addresses" to hide the receiver and "ring signatures" to hide the sender. The part that creates the most significant trade-off is the ring-signature system. Basically, a ring signature says "this transaction was sent by *one* of these 16 users, but you can't know exactly which one." One of those 16 users is the "real" sender, the other 15 are decoys. Because every transaction in the ledger is like that, you technically never know for certain if a particular user has ever sent *any* transactions. They might have just been used by someone else as a decoy every time they appear in the ledger. That approach is great for preserving privacy, but it's that same feature that means it is very difficult to prune data from the ledger, leading to scaling difficulties.

Coins like Grin use a privacy strategy called "MimbleWimble" (named after a spell from the Harry Potter universe). MimbleWimble is interesting because, in contrast to Monero, it actually makes it *easier* to prune data from the ledger. Large groups of transactions can be merged into a single big transaction and stored that way, allowing the intermediate data to be discarded. This makes MimbleWimble coins very scalable. But it comes with two key trade-offs. MimbleWimble naturally hides the transaction amount and the identity of the receiver, but it does not do much to hide the identity of the sender. If I send you coins in a MimbleWimble system, it's then easy for me to see when you spend the coins that I sent to you. If you take the coins that I sent to you and you send them to Charlie, then Charlie sends them to me, I can see that full sequence of transactions. Because I can trace the source of Charlie's coins to a point that I can identify (the transaction where I sent coins to you), I can then deduce that you must have had dealings with Charlie. Even though I can't see amounts or addresses, I can still learn some information about who you are connected to in the economy. Hiding the amounts and the receivers is a good start, but it's not quite as robust as privacy systems that also obscure the sender.

This finally brings us to mixing protocols for open ledgers. Most cryptocurrencies today have an open ledger. This includes all versions of Bitcoin and also Nano, Litecoin, Doge, Dash and really the vast majority of coins on the market today. In these ledgers, the amount, the receiver and the sender are all entirely public. Granted, the sender and receiver addresses are just random strings of text. But once you are able to associate an address to a real world identity, you can then see basically everything that person is doing with their funds. However, there are a few different technologies used to provide some rudimentary level of privacy in these systems. The main technology used for this purpose is a coin mixer. Examples of this type of tech include Samourai Wallet (for Bitcoin), CashFusion (for Bitcoin Cash), NanoFusion (for Nano), and PrivateSend (for Dash). A mixer is basically where a bunch of people all send their funds into a single account/address and then the funds are sent back out to fresh new addresses (often divided up into different amounts) belonging to the original owners. This obscures the trail of transactions. It's not really possible to tell which senders are connected to which receivers after the mix. This is fine as far as it goes, but there's a problem. It's pretty easy to deanonymize the mix if you have access to some metadata about the participants. For example, if you are making regular payments to a known address (like a café where you predictably buy coffee every morning), then the mixer won't help you much. Once you start using your mixed coins at the café, it will be clear to someone snooping on you that those are your coins, because they know what spending patterns to look for. Mixers are better than nothing, and they may stop some casual snooping by average people, but professional data miners (like the ones at Facebook,

Google or the NSA) will probably still be able to gather a significant amount of information about your spending habits.

The big question though: how do these privacy considerations play into our investment thesis?

It depends how big of a deal you think privacy features will be to future cryptocurrency adopters. Virtually every privacy feature comes with a significant trade-off in user experience. In Monero, mobile wallets often need to synchronise with the network for several minutes before you can make a transaction. In Grin, wallets need to be online in order to receive funds (you can't receive money passively while your wallet is offline). These are pain points for mass adoption and people will only tolerate them if they think their privacy is more valuable than the inconvenience.

If you think that most people are going to basically be fine with having their transaction history be traceable (the way they are pretty much fine with having a detailed snapshot of their personal info up on social media), then it makes sense not to worry too much about privacy features. You will lean towards coins that focus on a smooth user experience and don't worry as much about privacy.

If you think that people are going to value their financial privacy more in the future than they do today (which may well be the case if the government starts pushing CBDCs and tries to phase out physical cash), then you will want more privacy-focused coins in your portfolio.

 As an investor, you have to evaluate the privacy features, understand the user experience trade-offs, and allocate your portfolio based on your own personal forecast about which trade-offs the masses of everyday users are likely to favour.

## Does It *Need* to Be Decentralised?

This is a key technical question that you need to ask about any crypto project. Does the network around this project actually need to be decentralised? There are many projects out there that are just using "decentralised" and "blockchain" as buzzwords to get attention. But the product they are creating doesn't actually *need* to be decentralised in order to accomplish their goal. We talked about this in a previous chapter when we considered the possibility of a cryptocurrency token that would represent ounces of gold or silver in a vault. While this may seem like a neat idea, it doesn't solve the fundamental problem that has plagued the gold standard in the past: fractional reserves. If someone just gives you a crypto token, you have no way of knowing whether there is really physical metal in the vault to back it up. The owner of the vault might be issuing extra tokens with no actual metal behind them.

The addition of a decentralised crypto token does not remove the need to *trust* the vault owner. If the need for trust is not removed, then the decentralisation serves no purpose. The vault owner could give you an IOU scribbled on a scrap of paper and it would serve the same function. Or, more importantly, they could use a traditional *centralised* database where they record the ownership of all the metal in their vault. A centralised database is dramatically cheaper and easier to maintain than a decentralised network. Suppose two vault owners offer to run a gold-backed currency and one of them uses a centralised database while the other tries to represent their gold via a decentralised crypto token. The one using the centralised database will have much lower overhead costs, and therefore will be able to offer much lower fees to users for storing their metal and facilitating transactions. So in principle, the vault owner using the centralised database should out-compete the vault owner trying to use a decentralised token. The extra cost of using a decentralised network to store data is only justified if there is some benefit, namely, removing trust. If the terms of the arrangement mean trust is still required, then the decentralised network provides no extra value, only extra costs. For this reason, it does not make economic sense to put tokens for decentralised crypto networks in our portfolio if they don't solve the problem of removing trust from a system.

So then, what kinds of systems are genuinely able to have trust removed? The only systems that can have trust removed through a decentralised network are systems where the value is internal to the network itself. If the value of the network is tied to anything external, there is still a point of trust and the decentralisation is pointless. For this reason, decentralised tokens that represent physical commodities, real estate, company stocks, etc. don't really make sense. Those types of assets are better off using a centralised database which makes it clear *whom* you must trust. At least then you are going in with eyes wide open. This is also true of decentralised tokens which represent things like digital items inside a video game. If the item is only useful inside the game, and the game is controlled by its creators, then the token has no value without trusting the creators of the game. It would be better if the game creators just stored the ownership ledger of in-game items on their own systems. Since you have to trust the game creators either way, the players are better off having their in-game items stored efficiently on the game creators' centralised servers. This keeps network and storage costs are much lower, which alleviates any need to pay fees to node operators for transferring ownership within the ledger.

The one obvious use case for decentralisation is *money*. This is part of why my personal crypto portfolio is entirely focused on assets that are trying to function as digital cash. The purpose of owning these tokens is purely to allow you to transact *within* the network on which they exist. That's all. I buy them because I want the ability to do business with other people who want to use the same network. Facilitating those exchanges has value, regardless of anything else outside the crypto network itself.

There may be a handful of other uses for decentralised tokens that are not strictly "money". But they are very few and far between. I have heard of a couple of different attempts to build decentralised search engines where users earn tokens by using their compute power to provide search results to other users. They can use those tokens to gain privileges, such as deciding what ads are displayed beside search results within the network. Since this is all internal to the network, it potentially makes sense to decentralise. It can be trustless, at least in theory. I'm keeping my eye on this technology space, but haven't put any such tokens in my portfolio for now. It's the "money" use case that is much more interesting to me personally. As far as I can see, from an engineering standpoint, just about everything else in the crypto scene would be better off using a centralised system.

## Who Are the Major Competitors in This Niche?

One last major question to ask yourself before adding a cryptocurrency to your portfolio is how it stacks up against its most closely related competitors. Most cryptocurrency projects are "open source", meaning the source code to the software is freely available to anyone. In fact, any that are not open source should be avoided like the plague (why would you ever use a money system whose inner workings are a secret?!). But, because they are open, they are frequently copied. This is generally harmless. Interested computer programmers can make their own version of an existing cryptocurrency so that they can try out newer and more experimental ideas.

For example, there is a coin called Banano, which is basically a banana-and-monkey themed clone of Nano. Nano and Banano are pretty much the same in terms of their inner workings. But Nano is the actual serious competitor. Banano is a self-acknowledged clone for playing around with, not for serious business. The same is true of Wownero, which is a cloned version of Monero with some experimental features being tested.

There's nothing wrong with these projects per se, but it would be foolish for an investor who is looking to buy a privacy coin to choose Wownero instead of Monero. No one in either community is realistically expecting Wownero to replace Monero in real-world usage.

If you are looking at a coin, you need to understand what niche it is fitting into. Is it optimising for high transaction throughput? Low transaction fees? Privacy? Is it optimising for the easiest, smoothest payment experience? Whatever niche it is optimising for, make sure that you compare it to other coins which are also optimising for that same niche. If the coin you are considering doesn't come out a winner in its own niche, then it is probably wise to avoid it. It's certainly not going to make up much ground in the areas for which it is *not* being optimised.

# The Author's Portfolio

At this point in the book, I have introduced you to a basic set of filters that you can use to determine whether a cryptocurrency needs to be kept *out* of a responsible portfolio. But I'm a big fan of not giving people advice unless I follow it myself. To that end, I want to give you a basic overview of my own portfolio so that you can see (a) that I'm practising what I preach; and (b) see a practical example of how I personally apply these filters.

In the first place, let's talk about my allocation. As I write this, cryptocurrency makes up around 15% of our family's total investment portfolio. Given that I am obviously a crypto enthusiast, that may seem very low. But it's simply a reflection of our family's capacity for risk. We hold most of our portfolio in assets with less risk (the house we live in, precious metals and dividend-paying stocks). My wife and I have two small children, both under two years of age. Seeing your whole portfolio take a 50% dip takes a big emotional toll. Seeing 15% of your portfolio take that dip is much easier to handle. Having a cautious allocation is part of how we make sure that we're emotionally stable and able to look after each other and our children. Your circumstances will be different to ours, no two families are in exactly the same situation. You should determine your allocations accordingly.

Once you've decided what percentage of your portfolio you want to allocate towards crypto in general, you then need to decide which crypto assets are worth your time. So after all my own research, which coins did I end up including in my crypto portfolio? I'm going to reveal them to you, but first one final reminder.

As per the disclaimer at the beginning of this book, nothing here should be taken as financial advice. I don't know you, I don't know your financial situation. I'm providing this information purely for educational purposes, to help you better understand the issues at play when evaluating crypto assets. By telling you what coins I hold, I'm telling about risks that I have personally chosen to take. But that does *not* mean that you should take those same risks. You must decide for yourself. Your decisions are your own and if you lose a bunch of money, it won't be my fault. I accept zero liability for your investment choices. Got it? Good. With the lawyers satisfied, let's proceed.

# What's Left After Applying *My* Filters?

So far, I have only encountered three cryptocurrencies which passed enough of my filters to get a place in my own portfolio. Those are Bitcoin Cash, Monero and Nano. None of them are perfect. None of them check absolutely all of my boxes. But, in my personal opinion, they have *enough* strengths that I could potentially see them achieving mass adoption.

## Bitcoin Cash

Bitcoin Cash is a great all around coin for everyday commerce. It's smooth and easy for transactions, both online and in person. It has great scalability properties and is relatively easy to integrate with advanced features (like M-of-N multi-signature accounts and smart contracts). It already has widespread adoption among retail merchants in many areas (including North Queensland, Slovenia, parts of East Asia, South America and a few Caribbean islands). It's been proven to work reliably and to be relatively easy to introduce to non-technical users. On the negative side, it is a clear-ledger coin, so the privacy features are somewhat basic.

## Monero

Monero is the current king of the privacy space, as proven by its consistent adoption on dark net markets. For users who value privacy, Monero is the obvious choice. The more users there are in a privacy coin network, the more private it becomes. The larger user base means that the "anonymity set" (the crowd of people among whom a user can hide) is larger. So Monero's network effect actually feeds on itself more aggressively than with other cryptocurrencies. On the down side, Monero's wallet experience is a lot less smooth than other "digital cash" solutions, especially on mobile devices. Over time, developers may be able to sand off some of those rough edges, but some of them are unavoidable due to Monero's fundamental privacy architecture. That may be a significant handicap for achieving mass adoption.

## Nano

Nano has the smoothest mobile wallet experience of any cryptocurrency that I have ever used (specifically in a wallet app called Natrium). It also has the huge draw card that transactions are instant and have absolutely zero fees (as opposed to Bitcoin Cash and Monero, where you must wait for payment confirmation and fees are a fraction of a cent). Instant transactions and zero fees are a huge boon for mass adoption. This is how normal people realistically expect digital products to work. Sending an email is free and instant, posting on Facebook or Instagram is free and instant, why shouldn't sending money be free and instant as well? Nano also has a great narrative for appeasing government regulators: it has no mining farms. Nano uses a tiny amount of electricity to power the network. This plays very well to the crowd who want to invest in "green" technology. However, on the down side, Nano has even less in the way of privacy features than other clear-ledger coins like Bitcoin Cash. The design of Nano tends to push people toward reusing the same address for every transaction (as opposed to Bitcoin Cash, where each transaction uses a new address by default). This makes the users' activity very easy to track. Work has been done to create a mixing layer for Nano, but it is not being actively used at the present. It is only alpha-stage software and has no proven track record. Overall, Nano is simply a less mature project than Bitcoin Cash or Monero. But it also has a much smaller market cap. So while Nano still has some significant room for technical improvements, it also has tremendous upside potential in terms of price movement. Nano presents a chance to get in earlier than you would with more established coins. Higher risk, maybe, but also higher rewards if it pans out.

As I said, none of these cryptocurrencies tick every box. If I was going to wait for a cryptocurrency that was perfect in every single dimension, then I would not own any at all. I have made the calculated choice to put these in my portfolio, even knowing their imperfections, because I think that they have already proven to be useful to an awful lot of people. I want to be in on the cryptographic monetary revolution. I want to live in a world where governments cannot print money and steal away our purchasing power. I want to live in a world where people can freely buy and sell without censorship and without borders. I believe cryptocurrency is our best hope for achieving that dream and many people are already beginning to live that dream through these specific coins. And yes, I want to make a profit by trying to be ahead of the curve.

I have chosen these coins for my portfolio because I consider them the best of what is available *today*, in spite of their flaws and trade-offs. But I am always re-evaluating, always watching to see if something better comes along.

# Some Coins That I Rejected

A portfolio of only three coins is pretty narrow. You may be wondering about some others, maybe even some that you personally like but which didn't make my list. In this section, I want to share a few coins that I seriously considered for inclusion in my portfolio, but which I ultimately rejected. You may design your filters a little differently to me. You may come to different conclusions than I do. Some of these coins might end up in your portfolio. But for me they narrowly missed making the grade (for now). I want to be clear that I am not sharing these cryptos to speak ill of them. These are not the "trash" projects that I spoke of earlier. These are the ones that I consider "good but not great".

## Grin

I really like Grin as a piece of technology. It strikes a pretty good balance between privacy and scalability, being roughly as scalable as Bitcoin Cash, but far more private. Not as private as Monero, but not too bad. What keeps me away from Grin to this day is that it is genuinely difficult to obtain. I haven't found any faucets. I haven't been able to buy it on any familiar exchanges. The only sources I know of are small boutique exchanges that I don't fully trust. For this reason, it fails my obtainability filter.

## Zcash

As mentioned previously, there's some innovative privacy technology coming out of this team, but the trusted setup and the issuance policy were deal breakers for me. I don't like holding a coin where a corporate entity gets a huge clip of the mining rewards regardless of what they do or do not produce.

## Firo (formerly Zcoin)

Firo has some ideas and heritage in common with Zcash, but it seems to be moving in the direction of more battle-tested cryptography and privacy technologies that no longer required the trusted setup (in particular, Lelantus Spark). This makes me much more interested in Firo than Zcash. However, I still think the issuance policy is a problem. Firo has a big cut of mining rewards going to the corporate entity behind the project.

## Pirate Chain

Pirate Chain is using basically the same technology as Zcash, but enforcing that all transactions must be private rather than having the privacy element be optional. This is important because when someone in the network reveals their transaction information, that inevitably leaks some information about their trading partners (which could be you!). I think this step towards mandatory privacy is a good thing. However, Pirate Chain still has the trusted setup. I'm also not a fan of their reliance on the Bitcoin chain to provide part of their security. This last point is not strictly a deal-breaker, but I'm definitely more comfortable with networks that are self-contained and don't depend on other cryptocurrencies for part of their functionality.

## Bitcoin (BTC)

Excluding Bitcoin from my portfolio is probably my most controversial move. There is certainly a case that *could* be made for including it. But that case is purely based on following the crowd. The reason to buy Bitcoin BTC is because lots of other people are buying it (that's why it has the highest market cap of any cryptocurrency). At a minimum, that means that it has significant network effect, wide availability and recognisable branding. This creates two flow-on effects.

First, some very large investors are basically forced to start with Bitcoin if they want to be in the cryptocurrency space. It's much easier for them to buy a million dollars worth of BTC (without moving the spot price too much) compared to buying a million dollars worth of a smaller cap coin like Nano.

Second, if a whole nation is going to adopt a cryptocurrency as their main currency, it needs to have enough liquidity to absorb all of that economic activity. For nations like El Salvador, Bitcoin may be the most obvious choice for a crypto they can use as legal tender just because of the market cap, regardless of technical limitations.

These reasons made me strongly consider including BTC in my portfolio. But I continue to be held back by two major issues. First, the user experience is terrible. Transactions on the main network are expensive and slow to confirm and they will only get worse as adoption grows. Transactions on the Lightning Network either cause a frustrating user experience around payment reliability or else require custodial solutions. BTC simply does not get a passing grade on my usability filter.

If BTC ever does become widely adopted, I think that it will be for one of two reasons. First, it might be because of a radical new technological innovation, which improves the user experience, but which *does not exist yet*. That's theoretically possible. But I am not willing to bet my portfolio on a technological change which hasn't even been theorised, let alone implemented. Second, BTC might become widely adopted because it is imposed from above by governments (as has been the case in El Salvador). Governments can pass laws that require people to accept BTC at their businesses, or they can force people to use BTC for paying their taxes. If this type of top-down push for BTC occurs, then it will almost certainly mean three things. First, it will mean that the vast majority of people will be using BTC through custodial platforms. Second, it will mean that using BTC outside of those custodial platforms is highly regulated and not easy to do. Third, it will mean that governments are extremely tempted to take advantage of that custodial situation to produce inflation through fractional reserves. There will be a lot of people who think that they have BTC, but they really just have a digital IOU from the government. I don't want that. I want to use sound money. That is, money where we transact peer-to-peer and where we don't tolerate arbitrary inflation.

A final consideration is about the investment upside. Part of the reason to have cryptocurrency in your portfolio is because of the potential for gigantic gains. Coins with a smaller market cap naturally provide more upside potential than BTC. In order to make 10X your money holding BTC, the market cap of BTC would need to overtake the market cap of gold at this point (the market cap of BTC is currently about 10% of the market cap of gold). In order to make 10X your money in another cryptocurrency (one which people actually find easy to adopt and use), that other cryptocurrency doesn't even have to catch up to Bitcoin's market cap, let alone gold's market cap. For example, Bitcoin Cash is about 1% of the market cap of BTC. It only needs to reach 10% of the market cap of BTC for a 10X return. Nano is about 0.05% of the market cap of BTC. To get a 10X return there would only require enough people to adopt Nano that it reaches 0.5% of the market cap of BTC today. That's a far more achievable sounding goal. Meanwhile, the longer BTC keeps rising in speculative market cap, the further it has to fall. If masses of people eventually do start adopting cryptocurrency in daily use, they will quickly realise (as I did) that BTC does not score very well on a usability test. My prediction is that when real usage starts to outpace pure speculation, people will rapidly find other coins more practical to use and BTC will begin losing market share. There's a long way to fall when you start at number one.

If you ask a BTC enthusiast what is the main reason to hold BTC, they will almost certainly tell you "because it has a fixed supply, which makes it a good store of value." The problem is that this advantage doesn't set BTC apart from the competition. The cryptocurrencies that I hold in my portfolio *all* have a fixed monetary policy, which cannot be changed. Two of them have a fixed supply just like BTC, while the other has a fixed tail emission. One of them (Bitcoin Cash) actually has *exactly the same* fixed-supply policy as BTC since they share common ancestry. So while I definitely like BTC's fixed monetary policy, that alone is not enough reason for me to buy it, because I can get those benefits from other coins that have passed my usability filter.

## Ethereum

After Bitcoin, Ethereum is usually considered the other major force in the crypto space. Ethereum is an extremely interesting and clever project. But I still don't have it in my portfolio.

The main reason is that Ethereum is *not* trying to be a form of money. It is not, strictly speaking, a crypto*currency.* Ethereum is a technology platform for decentralised computing. It is a way for people around the world who do not trust each other to agree on the result of running a computer program. I am primarily interested in cryptocurrencies that are trying to be some form of "digital cash". Those are the assets that are going to protect me from inflation and give me purchasing power as they increase in adoption. But being useful as "cash" is not the main problem that Ethereum is trying to solve. Some of the problems that Ethereum smart contract developers are working on solving are problems that I don't even fully understand. Who really needs a leveraged-credit-default-swap contract? You would need an extensive background in financial markets and derivative instruments just to properly understand the problems involved, let alone the solutions. Since I don't think we are ever going to live in a world where the general population will genuinely understand those things, I don't think Ethereum will ever be as widely adopted (in real usage, not speculation) as competing cryptocurrencies that are simply trying to be an optimal form of "cash".

Aside from the issue of average people not even understanding the purpose of various Ethereum contracts, there is also the question of whether many of them actually *need* to be decentralised. To my mind, if a smart contract depends on "oracle" data from a trusted source (outside of the Ethereum network itself) then the problem addressed by that smart contract could almost certainly be done more efficiently on a centralised system. If you have to trust the oracle, then you have a single point of failure and you might as well embrace a system that makes the trust relationship clear and explicit.

For people who are really interested in decentralised finance (or "DeFi"), there is an awful lot going on in that space. It's just not that interesting to me for the reasons outlined above. There aren't enough hours in the day to be an expert on every subject, and I have chosen not to become an expert on complex smart contracts. I also don't have a problem with passing on investment opportunities that I don't really understand (even if they might be lucrative). Investing in things you fundamentally don't understand is just too risky for my taste. If you are interested in the DeFi space and feel that you understand it quite well, go ahead and add some DeFi projects to your portfolio. But I've decided that it's not for me.

## Dash

I have many excellent things to say about Dash. Most of the positive things that I would say about Bitcoin Cash are also true of Dash. They are similar in many ways. Dash has a smooth user experience for day-to-day transactions. This is born out by the large number of people who use Dash for day-to-day purchases in hotspots like New Hampshire and parts of Latin America.

For me, the deal breakers with Dash are the governance, the issuance policy and the competition.

For fans of Dash, the governance structure is often a selling point. There is a portion of each block reward set aside for things like development and marketing. In the Dash network, this fund is allocated to particular people by community members voting. The community members who get a vote are those who run "master nodes". To run a master node requires a large amount of Dash coins put up as collateral. The theory is that people running a master node have a large amount of Dash, so they are incentivised to see the network grow and stay healthy. By voting for whatever is best for the network, they are enabling their personal holdings to increase in value (or at least hold steady).

For people who favour that governance model, that design might be seen as a positive. However, I personally prefer the model where people simply pay for things that they want to see happen using their own money, rather than voting on how other people's money should be spent. There are various philosophical reasons why I prefer this model, which I won't go into here, but it is up to you to decide whether you agree or not.

The other big reason that I have not focused on Dash is because of the competition. Dash fills an extremely similar market niche to Bitcoin Cash. It is trying to provide for the "electronic cash" use case. Dash does this by having fast transactions, low fees and high scalability. It is a clear ledger with optional mixing-based privacy. These are all things I could equally say about Bitcoin Cash. But as things stand, the market cap of Bitcoin Cash is 6-7 times larger than that of Dash. My perception is that Bitcoin Cash is simply outstripping Dash in real-world adoption for this niche. If I wanted to be extra cautious, I could hedge my bets by adding Dash to my portfolio as well, but I think I'm already backing the winner in this niche by holding Bitcoin Cash.

# Conclusion: Risk Versus Reward

If you've read this far, congratulations. You have done more due diligence on understanding cryptocurrency than the vast majority of speculators in the market today. You've learned the fundamental value proposition of crypto: it's a form of money that makes it very easy to transact and very difficult to inflate. You've learned why inflation is such a big problem and why it's worth doing something to stop it.

You've considered the real risks that come with this highly speculative and volatile market. You've thought about what level of adoption in the global transaction market would be required for your speculations on a particular cryptocurrency to pay off. You've considered how large of an allocation to crypto is appropriate for your personal level of risk tolerance.

You've stepped through an example framework of filters for deciding whether a given crypto is worth your consideration. Those filters again, just to recap were the following:

- How difficult is it to *actually use?*

- Can I spend it somewhere?

- Is the issuance policy acceptable?

- What are the *internal* political risks?

- What are the *external* political risks?

- What are the technical risks?

- How private are my transactions?

- Does it *need* to be decentralised?

- Who are the major competitors in this niche?

You've seen some worked examples of how I apply these filters myself. You may disagree and design your own filters. You may have different preferences and different levels of risk tolerance. But this should have at least given you some food for thought.

My hope and prayer is that this book will have prepared you to make wise and well-informed decisions about the crypto market. From here, it is up to you. All investment and speculation activity comes with risk, this is just a part of life. Only God knows the future, including the future of financial markets. If the Lord God does see fit to bless you with a degree of wealth, my prayer is that He will also give you the ability to handle it well, so that it abounds to your good and ultimately to His glory.

Two things I have asked of you.
  Don't deny me before I die.

Remove far from me falsehood
and lies.
  Give me neither poverty nor
riches.

Feed me with the food that is
needful for me,
  lest I be full, deny you, and say,
'Who is the LORD?'

or lest I be poor, and steal,
  and so dishonour the name of
my God.

**Proverbs 30:7-10**

If you would like to go even deeper, additional
resources are available by visiting
https://www.cryptoforconservatives.com.

# Appendix 1: Knowing *When* to Buy and Sell

This book has been all about fundamental analysis, that is, knowing *what* to buy. But in highly speculative markets, it is also very important to consider "technical analysis", that is, knowing *when* to buy.

Technical analysts look at charts of asset prices and search for known patterns to try and discern what the broad mass of other investors are doing. By watching the price charts, we can see when investor sentiment is turning for or against any given asset. To some degree, analysts can use those patterns to predict when the price is likely to go up or down in the short-to-medium term. Any technical analyst will tell you that this is not an exact science. It's a game of probabilities and risk management. But because the crypto market is so speculative, it is a very useful tool.

There are times when the crypto market is clearly in a "mania" phase. Everybody and their dog seems to be buying everything in sight and prices are through the roof, even on crypto projects with poor fundamentals. This mania usually doesn't last long and is often followed by a huge price correction of

50% or more. This is somewhat normal. It's just the mass of buyers and sellers in the market coming to their senses and returning prices to more rational and realistic levels.

But even if you buy the absolute most solid assets in the crypto market, if you buy them at the top of a mania phase, then you could still lose a lot of money in the eventual correction. Learning how to time your purchases can help you avoid this problem.

Technical analysis is beyond the scope of this book. But there are resources on this topic available at https://www.cryptoforconservatives.com/technical-analysis.

# Appendix 2: Understanding the Word "Inflation"

Today's economists use the word "inflation" with multiple different meanings. Sadly, when you listen to them, they seem to be really bad at clarifying which one they are using. While academic economists may have other subtle definitions for the word "inflation", there are basically only two common meanings that concern us here.

The first common meaning is "an artificial increase in the supply of money". That is the meaning I have tried to use consistently throughout this book.

The second common meaning is "an increase in the prices of goods and services". When people talk about a rise in the "CPI" (consumer price index), this is what they are talking about. A loaf of bread was $3 last year and now it is $3.30.

When the supply of money gets increased, that usually causes a rise in prices over time. So the first meaning of "inflation" is the cause (the increase in the money supply) while the second meaning of "inflation" is the effect (rising prices).

The root cause of the confusion is that economists often use the same word "inflation" to refer to both the cause *and* the effect.

The problem with referring to rising prices as "inflation" is that prices of goods and services can change for all sorts of reasons. Suppose that we had a terrible bushfire season and lots of wheat got burned up. The supply of wheat for the year has fallen. If demand for wheat remains the same, then the price of wheat (and wheat-based products like bread) will go up in accordance with the laws of supply and demand. So prices would go up even though the money supply had not changed. Is that really "inflation"? I don't think so. It's just the market doing its thing by adjusting prices to various changes in supply and demand.

Now, in general, we would expect an increase in the money supply to cause a rise in the prices of goods and services. All else being equal, if there are more dollars chasing the same amount of goods and services then the prices of those goods and services will rise. Just like the wheat being burned up, the change in prices is simply a result of a change in supply and demand. The supply of dollars has increased. The supply of goods and services has not. This creates an imbalance. The prices of goods and services measured in dollars then rises in order to restore that balance. The rise in prices resulting from an increase in the money supply is no different from changes in prices that result from any other events in the economy.

For that reason, I prefer to reserve the term "inflation" for referring to the *cause* rather than the effect. It is not the rise in prices itself that steals your purchasing power, that creates the Cantillon effect, that suppresses interest rates and that triggers the boom-bust cycle. The rise in prices is just the market signalling to you that those things have already happened. It is the creation of new money by governments and central banks that causes those injustices. It is those injustices that cryptocurrency is designed to eliminate.